Fading Lines, Unfading Hope

Fading Lines, Unfading Hope

... And 30 Other Bible-Based Meditations

Roger Ellsworth

Unless otherwise noted, Scripture quotations are taken from the New King James Version®. Copyright © 1982 by Thomas Nelson. Used by permission. All rights reserved.

Copyright © 2017, Roger Ellsworth

All rights reserved. No part of this book may be reproduced, scanned, or distributed in any printed or electronic form without permission.

First Edition: 2017

ISBN: 978-0-9996559-1-7

20171212LSI

Great Writing Publications
www.greatwriting.org
Taylors, SC

www.greatwriting.org

Purpose

My Coffee Cup Meditations are short, easy-to-read, engagingly presented devotions based on the Bible, the Word of God. Each reading takes a single idea or theme and develops it in a thought-provoking way so that you are inspired to consider the greatness of God, the relevance of the good news of the life, death, resurrection, and coming-again of Jesus, and are better equipped for life in this world and well prepared for the world to come.

www.mycoffeecupmeditations.com

https://www.facebook.com/MyCoffeeCupMeditations/

Dedication

In memory of my dear brother in Christ

John Willis

and in appreciation for

Jackie Willis

Jamie and Joy Willis

Ryan and Tara Willis

Mitzie and Matt Bowlby

About This Book

This book is the result of the labors Roger Ellsworth and the thought he has given to various passages of Scripture over the years. You may read more about Roger on page 141.

We hope you will enjoy these Bible-based meditations. We would love to hear from you, so please send us a note to tell us what you think—which ones you liked most, and how they made a difference in your life or in the life of a family member, friend, or work associate. To reach us online, go to
www.mycoffeecupmeditations.com/contact

Table of Contents

1 Fading Lines, Unfading Hope 16
2 The Old Corn-Sheller 20
3 Needed: An Overpowering Love (1) 24
4 Needed: An Overpowering Love (2) 28
5 Albert Whitten's Pond 32
6 Great Things from a Special Visit 36
7 The "True!" Man 40
8 Mr. Firm in Faith 44
9 Brother Ernie and the Hornet 48
10 A "Bliss"ful Thought 52
11 Mr. Walking with God 56
12 Two Men and Three M's 60
13 Something to Be Said for God 64
14 Good Things from a Good Man 68
15 Mr. First in Heaven 72
16 Just Call Me a Christian 76
17 The Sluggard's Garden 80
18 Dining on the White of an Egg 84
19 Dogs That Won't Bark 88
20 The Day the Prayer-Shamers Will Pray 92
21 Sowing and Reaping 96
22 Moms and Mysteries 100
23 The Song of the Severed Arm 104
24 The Joyful Journey 108
25 The Precious Last Word 112

26 The Stork 116
27 The Language of Yesteryear 120
28 The Coppersmith and the Lord 124
29 Laughter, Bad and Good 128
30 A Pencil Stub and a Lemon Crate 132
31 What a Way to Live! What a Way to Die! 136

About the Author 140

The App

www.mycoffeecupmeditations.com

Be sure you get the app—coming soon. . .

-1-

From God's Word, the Bible...

Blessed be the God and Father of our Lord Jesus Christ, who according to His abundant mercy has begotten us again to a living hope through the resurrection of Jesus Christ from the dead, to an inheritance incorruptible and undefiled and that does not fade away, reserved in heaven for you, who are kept by the power of God through faith for salvation ready to be revealed in the last time.

1 Peter 1:3-5

Fading Lines, Unfading Hope

We had to spend quite a bit of time in the barn on the little family farm that I called home during my childhood years. The cows had to be milked each morning and evening.

That barn was already old and rickety when my dad bought the farm. In wintertime the wind would whistle through the cracks in those barn walls and chill us to the bone.

My dad's remedy for the problem was to nail cardboard over those cracks. That certainly didn't make the barn cozy and warm, but it helped.

That cardboard became precious to me. Precious cardboard? It sounds ridiculous, doesn't it?

The preciousness of it had nothing to do with it knocking down the frigid blasts of the wintry wind. It rather had to do with the sketches my dad drew on it. He had been reading the Apostle John's description of the throne room of heaven in the fourth and fifth chapters of Revelation, and he was so excited about what he read that he just had to share it. So he took the pencil that he invariably carried in the bib of his overalls and drew a couple of diagrams on the cardboard.

My dad died on August 4, 1985. When I went home for his funeral, I suddenly found myself thinking about those sketches. So I walked out to the old barn, which was now even more weary and rickety. The cardboard was still there. I brushed away the cobwebs and dirt, and there were dad's sketches. The lines were now faint and faded, but I could still make them out.

As I stood there gazing at lines drawn so many years ago, a couple of things came to mind. One was how very blessed I was to have a father who believed and practiced these words: "And these words which I command you today shall be in your heart; you shall teach them diligently to your children, and shall talk of them when you sit in your house, when you walk by the way, when you lie down, and when you rise up" (Deut. 6:6-7).

We seem to have little trouble passing our political views on to our children. And we do very well in passing on to our children our allegiance to various sports and teams. But how are we doing in passing spiritual things on to our children? Christian parents should give priority to talking to their children about:

- their faith and why they hold it;
- their life and how they have made it;
- their hope and how they prize it.

And if we have been blessed with such parents, we should daily give thanks to the Lord in heaven.

I also found myself thinking that day about the hope that those faint lines represented—the hope of heaven!

The word "hope" has lost some of its weight over the years. When we say we are hoping for something, there is an element of uncertainty. We're not sure that the thing we're hoping for is going to be the case.

When the Bible uses the word "hope," there is no uncertainty. Hope is rather being so convinced that something is true that we stand on our tiptoes and crane our necks to see it. The Christian's hope is "both sure and steadfast" (Heb. 6:19).

So the Christian doesn't wonder if heaven is a reality. He or she knows it is and looks forward to it with eager expectation.

Dad's lines had become very faint when I last saw them in 1985, and now they, and the old barn, are gone. But the hope of heaven is not faint, and it is not gone. My dad's soul is already with the Lord in heaven, and one glorious day the Lord Jesus will bring that soul with Him, will raise my dad's body from the grave, rejoin it with his soul, and he and all God's children will be forever with the Lord in "a new heaven and a new earth" (Rev. 21:1).

I'm glad my dad treasured that hope while he was on this earth, and God used him to help me treasure it as well. Do you, too, have an unfading and certain hope for heaven?

-2-

From God's Word, the Bible...

And they continued steadfastly in the apostles' doctrine and fellowship, in the breaking of bread, and in prayers.

Acts 2:42

The Old Corn-Sheller

Growing up on our small family farm in southern Illinois meant daily chores for my brother and me. The cows had to be brought in from the pasture, fed, and milked. The hogs had to be "slopped." The chickens had to be fed, and eggs had to be gathered.

We often fed the chickens shelled corn. The corn-sheller was an odd-looking thing. It had a cone shaped device at the top into which we fed ears of corn. As we pressed each ear into that cone, we would turn the large handle on the side of the machine. That pressing and turning would force the ears between two large wheels with iron teeth, one turning one direction and the other in the opposite direction. Those wheels would remove the kernels of corn from the cob. The kernels would be funneled through a chute into a bucket and the corncobs would fall into a compartment at the bottom.

It was a tedious process. The shucks had to be removed from the ears of corn before the actual shelling began. And only one ear of corn could be shelled at a time. Simultaneously pressing the ear into the cone and turning the handle was something of a test of coordination. But the process was effective. As the shelled corn was scattered around on the ground, the chickens would eagerly gather and eat. If they had known about the tedium, they wouldn't have cared. All that mattered to them was the tasty meal produced by it.

The knack to doing good things that are tedious in nature is to keep in mind the good produced by them. The cornsheller helped to feed the chickens, and those chickens helped to feed us! The tedium produced good things!

The Bible is the most wonderful book to ever come into human hands. It has God for its author, the Lord Jesus as its focus, salvation for sinners as its theme, and eternal glory in heaven as its end. But the wonderful nature of the Bible doesn't prevent tedium from setting in as we read and study it. The more familiar we are with the Bible, the more likely we are to experience slowness and sluggishness in the handling of it. It ought always to thrill us, but sometimes it doesn't.

How are we to combat the tedium that comes from familiarity with the Bible? By reflecting on what a wonderful thing it is and by remembering the good that it produces. Even when Bible reading is laborious, the Bible is doing its work in us by building up our spiritual strength and increasing our faith.

Prayer can become tedious. We set for ourselves the discipline to pray, and before we know it we find ourselves merely saying words, hurrying to get through, and promising ourselves that we'll be more engaged next time. All of this comes about because we so easily lose sight of the wonder of prayer. Think about it! We speak on earth, and our Father in heaven bends His ear to listen! The good produced by prayer is immeasurable. We are brought close to God and given strength to face life's demands. We learn to rest in

God's will and to trust in His guidance. And we come to appreciate more the Lord Jesus. Praying makes us realize — at at least, it should — that prayer itself is a privilege purchased for us at a dear cost.

And that cost? The death of Christ on the cross! We have never adequately understood Christ's death if we think of it in physical terms alone. It was much more than that! The Lord Jesus actually received on the cross the wrath of God in the place of sinners so that all who trust in Him in His death never have to receive that wrath themselves. Through that death, we are made right with God and given access to God through prayer.

As the tedium of corn shelling produced good results for the chickens and for our family, so the tedium of Bible study and prayer will produce good results for us. So get to shelling!

.

-3-

From God's Word, the Bible...

He who loves father or mother more than Me is not worthy of Me. And he who loves son or daughter more than Me is not worthy of Me.

Matthew 10:37

So when they had eaten breakfast, Jesus said to Simon Peter, "Simon, son of Jonah, do you love Me more than these?" He said to Him, "Yes, Lord; You know that I love You." He said to him, "Feed My lambs."

John 21:15

Needed: An Overpowering Love (1)

One of the things that concern me most about the current generation of Christians is the absence of what I will call an overpowering love. I'm talking about a love that is so mighty that it subdues and conquers other loves. More particularly, I'm talking about a love for the Lord that is so fervent and passionate that it drives out of our lives things that we shouldn't love at all, and properly orders things that we shouldn't love as much as we do.

There are things we shouldn't love at all. Take pornography for example. Recent surveys not only indicate that a very large percentage of Christian men regularly visit pornographic sites but also that a high percentage of pastors do as well. What is lacking is a love for the Lord that is so powerful that it drives out this thing that should have no place at all—a love for the Lord that is so strong that the Christian man can say to the devil: "Tempt me all you want, I am not going to yield!"

That kind of love for Christ seems to be increasingly rare these days.

Then there are those things that we shouldn't love as much as we do. It's okay to have a love for them, but they are not to be loved to the degree that they often are. Sports may be the best example of this. There is nothing wrong with having an interest in baseball, football, basketball, and golf, but Christians very often allow their interest in sports to override everything else. It's very common for Christians to excuse themselves from church services so they can attend a game or so their children can participate in one. And, increasingly it seems, this is viewed as a legitimate reason for skipping church.

I wonder where those Christians are who say this: "Yes, I love sports, but the Lord is my greatest love, and I will not put any other love above Him."

Many churches have abandoned Sunday evening services. The rationale that is often given is that this allows their members to spend time with their families.

And I wonder where those are who say this: "We certainly love our families, but we love the Lord—who gave us our families—even more." What better time to spend together as a family than being in church?

How did we arrive at the conclusion that Sunday evening is the only time we have to spend with our families? What happened to the other evenings?

So we are face to face with disturbing questions: Where is that love for Christ that is so powerful that it excludes false loves and properly aligns legitimate loves? Why is it that we don't love Christ more? Is it because we don't really understand what He has done for us? Is it because we think we can love Him without following His commandments? Or is the problem that many of us who think we are Christians have never been truly converted?

Yes, the world is so very alluring; the flesh is so very weak; and the devil so very strong and clever. But shouldn't there be in Christians something greater than the world, the flesh, and the devil? William R. Featherston evidently found it to be so:

> *My Jesus, I love Thee; I know Thou art mine.*
> *For Thee all the follies of sin I resign.*
> *My gracious Redeemer, my Savior art Thou.*
> *If ever I loved Thee, My Jesus 'tis now.*

Amazingly enough, Featherston penned these words when he was only sixteen years old. Born July 23, 1846, in Montreal, he came to know the Lord in Toronto in 1862. Shortly after, he wrote a poem to celebrate his conversion and mailed it to his aunt in Los Angeles. Somehow it was set to music and appeared in a British hymnal in 1864. Featherston himself was to have only ten years to walk on this earth with the Lord he so loved before actually meeting Him in glory at age twenty-six. These words indicate that he eagerly looked forward to that meeting:

> *In mansions of glory and endless delight,*
> *I'll ever adore Thee in heaven so bright.*
> *I'll sing with the glittering crown on my brow,*
> *"If ever I loved Thee, My Jesus 'tis now."*

-4-

From God's Word, the Bible...

But God forbid that I should boast except in the cross of our Lord Jesus Christ, by whom the world has been crucified to me, and I to the world.

Galatians 6:14

Needed: An Overpowering Love (2)

In the previous reading I registered my concern that there seems to be among today's Christians a lack of unusual love for the Lord—love so strong that it drives out of our lives false loves and puts in order legitimate loves.

So what is the way to have more love for Christ? Is it just a matter of one saying, "I need to love Christ more"? That would certainly be a good place to start! But realizing our need for it isn't enough in and of itself to take us there.

I have found over the years that the cross of Christ supplies the answer to my most perplexing questions and my most vexing problems.

The way to greater love for Christ, I suggest, is the way of the cross. It is to think more deeply about the cross than ever before.

Here are some lines from *The Ninety and Nine*, a poem written many years ago by Elizabeth C. Clephane:

> *But none of the ransomed ever knew*
> *How deep were the waters crossed;*
> *Nor how dark was the night*
> *That the Lord passed through*
> *Ere He found His sheep that was lost.*

If we could only get a better understanding of why Jesus was on the cross and what He did there! If we only knew "how deep were the waters crossed" and "how dark was the night" that He "passed through."

Many of us have been familiar with the cross for years. We have heard from childhood that Jesus died on the cross for our sins. How easily the words fall from our tongues!

But, oh, what sins! And, oh, what a death! Our love for Christ will be in direct proportion to the degree that we have plumbed the depths of both.

Sin seems to be a very light and trivial matter to most people, but it's nothing of the sort. Our sin is nothing less than an all-out assault on God Himself. It's essentially the creature hating the Creator and saying to Him, "I wish You were dead."

This is how serious sin is—it merits eternal separation from the God who is so holy that He cannot and will not dwell with sinners in eternity. Don't expect to find greater love for Christ apart from a better understanding of what a heinous, vile thing sin is.

It was our sin that brought Jesus to this earth in our humanity, and it was our sin that caused Him to go to the cross. We must never, never think of Jesus' death in physical terms only. There was much more going on while He was on that cross than a man dying physically. He was on that cross to pay the penalty for sinners, to receive what they deserve so they would not have to receive it. Jesus went to that cross as the propitiation for sinners. To propitiate is to appease or satisfy wrath. God has real wrath against our sins, and Jesus, by dying on that cross, satisfied the wrath of God. How so? He received that wrath in the place of sinners, and God, having poured out His wrath on Jesus, was propitiated. This was the "dark night" that Jesus "passed through." It was the dark night of the wrath of God (Matt. 27:45-46). And all that Jesus did on the cross counts for all who will repent of their sins and trust in Him. Believe on the Lord Jesus Christ, and you will be saved! (Acts 16:31).

The cross of Christ tells us what we have been saved *from* (sin and the wrath it deserves) and what we have been saved *by* (that is, Jesus bearing God's wrath in our stead). It also tells us what we have been saved *to*—eternal glory in heaven.

If we are believers in Christ, we have hell behind us and heaven in front of us! And it's all because of Jesus and what He did on the cross. Go over it and keep going over it until the ice melts in your heart and you can say with William R. Featherston:

> *I love Thee because Thou hast first loved me,*
> *And purchased my pardon on Calvary's tree.*

-5-

From God's Word, the Bible...

Therefore, being a prophet, and knowing that God had sworn with an oath to him that of the fruit of his body, according to the flesh, He would raise up the Christ to sit on his throne, he, foreseeing this, spoke concerning the resurrection of the Christ, that His soul was not left in Hades, nor did His flesh see corruption.

Acts 2:30-31

Albert Whitten's Pond

If I were asked to name the dearest places on earth to me, I would have to include Albert Whitten's pond. I'm convinced it was also one of the coldest places on earth—at least on one particular day.

The year was 1956, the month was April. The day was Sunday, the 8th. The time was shortly after the morning worship service of Bethel Baptist Church, a small rural church near Vandalia, Illinois.

I had found the Lord the preceding Sunday. Actually, it was the Lord who had found me, pardoned me, and saved me. Glory to His name!

Bethel church didn't have a baptistry, but she did have Albert's pond. Albert Whitten, a faithful member of the church, lived a mere half mile from the church. So that is where Bethel church did her baptizing.

The many years that have come and gone since that day have made vague many of its details. I remember my pastor, Burliss Hill, walking out into the water with a long stick in his hand to locate a place where the footing would be secure.

I remember the water being so cold that it almost took my breath away, and to this moment I can almost feel the heavy, calloused hand of my pastor, Burliss Hill, resting on my back. I remember the words he spoke: "I now baptize you, my brother, in the name of the Father, the Son, and the Holy Ghost." And I remember my mother rushing to wrap a warm quilt around me as I emerged from the pond.

On that day, I didn't have the theology of baptism as much in place as I do today. I'm glad one doesn't have to be perfect in theology in order to be saved and baptized. I did know that baptism did not save me. That came about as the Spirit of God gave me spiritual life and I trusted in the redeeming work of the Lord Jesus. So the front pew of Bethel Baptist Church where I knelt with my father and prayed for the Lord to save me will always be dearer to me than Albert's pond.

But baptism is important. It publicly identifies the believer with his or her Lord. It pictures outwardly what happens inwardly when a person is saved. Salvation is nothing less than dying to the old life of sin and being raised to walk with Christ in new life. Baptism depicts that. It pictures death, burial, and resurrection with Christ.

In my baptism I was giving visible testimony that the Lord had saved me and that I now belonged to Him. Albert Whitten's pond became a dear place because the Lord had become dear.

I don't know whether Albert Whitten's pond still exists. It may not. Someone may have filled it in and built a barn or a corn crib over it. But, thank God, my identification with the Lord—which baptism in that pond represented—still stands. When the Lord saves, it is forever.

I know that Albert himself and most of the others who gathered around that pond on that cold April day have passed off this earthly stage. Because the Lord's salvation lasts forever, they last as well. Physical death didn't put an end to their existence. Their souls are already with the Lord Jesus, and when He comes again, as He has promised to do, He will raise their bodies from their graves, fashion those bodies after His own resurrection body, and reunite those bodies with their souls. And all of God's people will dwell with the Lord forever in those new bodies and on a new earth. There we will not congregate around a farmer's pond but rather near the river of life (Rev. 22:1).

This wonderful future has been purchased for believers in Christ by the Lord Jesus in whom they believe. He purchased it for them by His death on the cross. So the dearest place in all of human history is the place where they dropped the cross of Jesus into a hole—that place where He died—that place where He cried out, "It is finished!" (John 19:30).

-6-

From God's Word, the Bible...

Then the LORD appeared to him by the terebinth trees of Mamre, as he was sitting in the tent door in the heat of the day. So he lifted his eyes and looked, and behold, three men were standing by him; and when he saw them, he ran from the tent door to meet them, and bowed himself to the ground, and said, "My Lord, if I have now found favor in Your sight, do not pass on by Your servant."

Genesis 18:1-3

Read the whole passage in Genesis 18.1-15.

Great Things from a Special Visit

Abraham had just settled down to enjoy a nap when he saw three men approaching. These were very special men and this was a very special visit.

I suggest that there are four very great things that emerge from this visit. First, there is *a great wonder to ponder*.

Here's how very special these men were—one was God in human flesh, and the other two were angels in human flesh! (vv. 13, 14, 16, 17, 22, 19:1).

This is utterly amazing. The eternal, sovereign, majestic, glorious God comes to Abraham as a man to sit at his table and to eat his food. This is a preview of the incarnation. For this visit, the Lord took humanity temporarily. Centuries later at Bethlehem, He would take it permanently.

We're so used to hearing about Jesus taking our flesh that it's easy to lose sight of the wonder of it. The Second Person of the Trinity walking among us! Eating our food! Drinking our drink! The incarnation is a great wonder indeed, but even greater is the wonder of Jesus taking our humanity to the cross where He received the wrath we deserve so we don't have to fear that wrath ourselves.

Here also is *a great prayer to pray*.

Abraham must have received a revelation from heaven that the Lord Himself was coming for a visit. So he ran to them and said: "My Lord, if I have found favor in Your sight, do not pass on by Your servant" (v. 3).

I'm not suggesting that the Lord appears to us in human flesh as He did to Abraham. But He visits with His people through His Spirit and His Word. How do we respond when we sense God is near? We should pray as Abraham did: "Lord, please don't pass us by."

If you aren't a Christian, you may sense God speaking to you today. Make this your prayer:

> *Pass me not, O gentle Savior*
> *Hear my humble cry.*
> *While on others Thou art calling,*
> *Do not pass me by.*

We also have here *a great quality to practice*. When Abraham realized he was receiving guests from heaven, he sprang into action. This old man acted as if he were young (vv. 2, 6, 7).

Abraham was eager both to receive the Lord and to serve the Lord. How eager are we when it comes to the things of God? Are we eager to worship, to pray, or to hear the Word of God?

Could it be that God doesn't come near more often because we're so slow and sluggish in spiritual things? The risen Christ rebuked two of His disciples for being "slow of heart" (Luke 24:25). Would He offer the same rebuke to us?

It's amazing how eager we are about sports, family gatherings and vacations, and how slow we are in the things of God.

This passage also shows us *a great danger to avoid*.

The Lord and His angels came to visit Abraham and Sarah to deliver a marvelous message. Although well advanced in years, Abraham and Sarah were going have a son! (v. 10). This would bring joy to Abraham and Sarah, but there was much more to it than that. This son would be the one through whom God would fulfill His promises to Abraham, the one from whom the Messiah would come.

When Sarah heard this, she laughed. It wasn't the laughter of rejoicing but rather the laughter of unbelief. At this moment, Sarah was an unbelieving believer.

What a sad thing it is to be an unbelieving believer! The greatness of our blessing hinges on the greatness of our faith. The preacher C. H. Spurgeon used to say: "Brethren, be great believers. Little faith will bring your souls to heaven, but great faith will bring heaven to your souls."

The Lord responded to Sarah's laughter by reminding her that nothing is too hard for Him (v. 14).

Faith is often attacked in these days. The way to fortify it is to feed it with the truth that nothing is too hard for our God. In due time, He will—by His mighty power—bring all things to the end that He has appointed. Then all will know that He is God. Until then, let us avoid the danger of being unbelieving believers.

-7-

From God's Word, the Bible...

Let the redeemed of the LORD say so,
Whom He has redeemed from the hand of the enemy,
And gathered out of the lands,
From the east and from the west,
From the north and from the south.

Psalm 107:2-3

The "True!" Man

The word "Amen" means "True." As far as I know Bob Brock had no dislike for the word "Amen," but he preferred "True!" And as I preached many years ago at First Baptist Church, Fairfield, Illinois, Bob would repeatedly say "True!" I'm glad he never found it necessary to cry out: "False!"

Some preachers (including the great Martyn Lloyd-Jones) have expressed displeasure at any vocal responses during preaching. I'm not among them. Bob's "True!' was always an encouragement to me. It told me that he was thinking along with me and that he was rejoicing in the Word of God. I can't help but think that God used his repeated use of "True!" to cause others to think seriously about spiritual things.

The tide is running against Christianity these days. Those who fancy themselves to be terribly enlightened look upon Christians with disdain and make little attempt to conceal it. They find it hard to believe that anyone with even modest intelligence could possibly embrace it. So why do we Christians insist on holding on to our faith? Why do we not abandon Christianity so we can be in step with the times? The answer lies in Bob Brock's word: "True!"

As its name indicates, Christianity is all about the Lord Jesus Christ. It is true that He was God in human flesh. He was the God-man, fully God and fully man at one and the same time. And He is the only One in all of human history of whom this can be said.

How do we know Jesus was the God-man? His miracles give testimony to His identity. During His public ministry, He did many miracles and many kinds of miracles. And these were witnessed by multitudes. The evidence for Jesus is so great that we don't have to be in any doubt about Him.

It is true that Jesus died on a Roman cross and was buried in the tomb of Joseph of Arimathea. It is also true that death could not hold Him. He sprang from it in glorious resurrection life on the third day just as He promised. How do we know He arose? The women who came to the tomb found the heavy stone was rolled away and the Roman guards were stupefied. Angels were present. The tomb was empty. The grave clothes were arranged in a convincing fashion. And the risen Christ began making appearances to His disciples—to five hundred at one time (1 Cor. 15:6). And the disciples were transformed from a band of whimpering cowards into bold evangelists.

It is also true that Jesus in His birth, life, death, and resurrection fulfilled many, many prophecies of the Old Testament. How many? Some put the number at 325! The mathematical probability that one man could coincidentally fulfill that many prophecies is astronomical stacked on astronomical.

The debate rages about Jesus today, but there is coming a day in which the debate will be over. The author of Hebrews says:

For yet a little while,
And He who is coming will come and will not tarry
(Heb. 10:37).

The Apostle John writes of Jesus: "Behold He is coming with clouds, and every eye will see Him, and they also who pierced Him. And all the tribes of the earth will mourn because of Him. Even so, Amen" (Rev. 1:7).

Everybody will know the truth about Jesus when He comes again.

Bob Brock died many years ago. I imagine his first conversation with the Lord may have gone something like this:

The Lord: "Bob, you were a great sinner."

Bob: "True!"

The Lord: "But I loved you even before the world began."

Bob: 'True!"

The Lord: "And I purchased your pardon with my precious blood on the cross of Calvary."

Bob: "True!"

The Lord: "Now enter into the joys and glories of what has been prepared for you."

Bob: "True! And hallelujah!"

When I meet Bob again in heaven's glory, I won't be surprised if he says to me: "By the grace of our Lord, you have made it safely home."

If he does, I know what I will say: "True!"

-8-

From God's Word, the Bible...

Then the LORD saw that the wickedness of man was great in the earth, and that every intent of the thoughts of his heart was only evil continually. And the LORD was sorry that He had made man on the earth, and He was grieved in His heart. So the LORD said, "I will destroy man whom I have created from the face of the earth, both man and beast, creeping thing and birds of the air, for I am sorry that I have made them." But Noah found grace in the eyes of the LORD.

Genesis 6:5-8

Read the whole passage: Genesis 6:1-8, 11-13.

Mr. Firm in Faith

What is it to be firm in faith? It means to believe the Word of God and to act upon it even when it seems to be absurd to do. Noah wasn't the only member of the family of faith to be firm in faith, but he was certainly firm in his faith.

Think about the message that Noah received. What a message it was! It was a message about sin, judgment to come, but also a way of escape.

Yes, it was a message about sin. Noah's world was godless in every respect (vv. 5, 11-12). People were corrupt. That means that they were not as God made them to be. They were violent (v. 11), and they went about the ordinary pursuits of life without giving any regard or heed to God (Luke 17:26-27).

That brings us to the judgment part of the message. God said He wasn't going to continue to put up with people's wickedness. He was rather going to bring it to a sudden and immediate halt by sending a great flood.

What a sorrowful message it would have been if it had

only been about sin and judgment! But it was also a message about escape or salvation. Noah was to build an ark to save himself, his family, and to ensure the future of the animal kingdom.

Think also about the difficulties Noah encountered. Perhaps no one has ever had more obstacles in the way of faith than Noah. Nature was against him. Early in Genesis we learn that the earth was watered by a mist that came up from the ground (Gen. 2:5-6). There had never been anything to suggest that a great flood would take place.

Society was also against Noah. No one agreed with him about this flood except his immediate family. His larger family didn't believe. His friends didn't believe. His business acquaintances didn't believe. Noah was virtually alone in his faith.

Time was also against him. One hundred and twenty years elapsed from the time that Noah received the message and began building the ark until the flood actually came. Faith often falters when there is a large gap between God's promise and its fulfillment. We are ever inclined to take delay to mean failure.

Finally, think about the response Noah offered. With everything and everyone against him, Noah clung to the Word of God. He believed the message he had received from God, and he acted upon it. Year after year went by and Noah worked on the ark and warned his fellow citizens about the judgment to come.

How was Noah able to be so firm in his faith? How could he go on believing when he had so many reasons for doubting? What he saw around him certainly confirmed the message from God. It was clear that people were just as sinful as God had said. Noah also knew of an instance of unprecedented supernatural activity in the world. God had taken his great grandfather Enoch directly from earth to heaven. But there was more. Noah could not help himself. Every time he was tempted not to believe, his faith would take over. Faith is God's gift, and God will always nurture it and sustain it.

What does it all have to do with us? We, like Noah, are called to believe a message from God that seems ridiculous. We are called to believe that men and women are still sinful by nature, and that God will finally bring eternal judgment upon them. We are also called to believe that there is a way of escape from the coming judgment. Noah and his family escaped the flood because of the ark. When the rain came pouring down, not one drop of it fell on them.

The Lord Jesus is our ark of safety in the face of the judgment to come. He went to the cross to receive the full storm of the wrath of God against sinners. All the wrath fell on him, and those who place faith in Him will never have to worry about one drop of God's wrath falling on them.

-9-

From God's Word, the Bible...

*. . . lest Satan should take advantage of us;
for we are not ignorant of his devices.*

2 Corinthians 2:11

Brother Ernie and the Hornet

One of the greatest challenges the preacher faces is distractions. Crying babies, coughing listeners, ringing cell phones, and people walking in and out are some of the most common.

The most unusual distraction that came my way was in the form of a wonderful deacon, Ernie Vogel. As I was preaching one Sunday morning in my first pastorate, Panama Baptist Church in Panama, Illinois, Brother Ernie suddenly rose from his seat and started walking toward me with a rolled-up Sunday School quarterly in his hand. I wondered if he was coming to the pulpit to smack me. Instead he veered to his right, stopped at a window, and proceeded to deliver four or five mighty blows to that window. Everyone was transfixed. What was he doing? We weren't in suspense very long. Brother Ernie turned to me, smiled and proudly said: "Preacher, there was a hornet over here, but don't worry. I got him."

With that, he returned to his seat and I tried to resume my sermon.

So Brother Ernie had dispatched a hornet into eternity in the middle of my sermon! If I had been on my toes, I would have pointed out how quickly life can end and we can be out in eternity!

I've never been very good at handling distractions while I'm preaching. I guess you could say that I find them to be, well, distracting. Once the attention of hearers is broken, it can be hard to get it back. And for one who preaches without notes, it can be hard to get back on track.

Things that distract from the preaching and hearing of God's Word are bad enough, but those things that distract us from life's main business are even worse. And what is life's main business? It is receiving forgiveness from God for our sins, living for His glory, and going to heaven when we die.

What are some of the things that distract us from this business? We can begin with things. We can become so absorbed with our pursuit of material things that we do not give due diligence to spiritual things. In His parable of the sower and the different kinds of soil, Jesus warned about the "thorny-ground" hearer who has the Word choked out by "the cares of this world and the deceitfulness of riches" (Matt. 13:22).

Preoccupation with material things can keep us out of the kingdom of God—that is the point Jesus was making—but it can also get a foothold in the Christian life.

We can also be distracted from life's main business by people. After His resurrection, the Lord Jesus sought out Simon Peter to recommission him. Part of that recommissioning consisted of Jesus telling Simon that he would have to lay down his life for the sake of his Master. Simon responded by asking Jesus: "But Lord, what about this man?"

Simon was referring to his fellow-disciple, John. Jesus responded, saying, "If I will that he remain till I come, what is that to you? You follow Me" (John 21:15-25).

Peter was allowing himself to be distracted by John, but Jesus called him back to his business, which was to follow the Lord.

How easy it is for us to become slack in our service to the Lord because of someone else! Perhaps someone in whom we had great confidence ended up disappointing us; perhaps another person has received more acclaim for his or her service than we have for ours. No matter how poor or how good the performance of others is, we must not allow ourselves to be distracted by them. Our business is not to concern ourselves with the business of others. Our business is to follow the Lord.

Space doesn't allow me to deal with other distractions—interest in sports and pleasures, killing time on the Internet, etc.

All things that distract us from service to the Lord come from the devil. He is the master-distracter. If he can't keep us from coming to the Lord, he will certainly do all he can to keep us from serving as effectively as we should. Let's make sure we are not ignorant of his devices.

-10-

From God's Word, the Bible...

But God demonstrates His own love toward us, in that while we were still sinners, Christ died for us.

Romans 5:8

. . . so Christ was offered once to bear the sins of many. To those who eagerly wait for Him He will appear a second time, apart from sin, for salvation.

Hebrews 9:28

A "Bliss"ful Thought

Philip Bliss and his wife died in a train wreck on December 29, 1876. The train was nearing Ashtabula, Ohio, when the trestle it was crossing collapsed. Bliss escaped without injury but perished in the ensuing fire as he tried to free his trapped wife. He was thirty-eight years old.

Bliss was a remarkably gifted hymn-writer and singer. When we hear his name, those of us who know our hymns easily think of *Wonderful Words of Life, Hallelujah! What a Savior!, Almost Persuaded, Jesus Loves Even Me,* and *I Will Sing of My Redeemer*. He also wrote the music for Horatio Spafford's hymn *It Is Well with My Soul*.

One of his lesser-known hymns is *Once for All*. This hymn begins with this "Bliss"-ful thought:

> *Free from the law, O happy condition,*
> *Jesus hath bled, and there is remission; …*

Very few seem to realize that God Himself is holy and that He demands that we be perfectly holy before He will allow us to enter into heaven. What is perfect holiness? It is conforming to the law of God in every respect. And what is the law of God? It is His moral law that we find perfectly expressed in the Ten Commandments. If we could keep those commandments, we would have the perfection that God demands. But, alas, we don't keep them. Even before we learn about God's law, we have already broken it time after time! After we learn about it, we continue to break it. So God's law can never save us. It can only show us how sinful we are. The law of God can never pronounce us justified in the eyes of God. It rather pronounces us condemned.

Go through the Ten Commandments one by one, and each one will shout "Guilty!" at you. Not one will shout "Not guilty!"

Violating God's law carries a penalty with it, and the penalty is terrible beyond measure. It is eternal separation from God. That penalty has to be paid. God can't just set it aside. If He were to do so, He would not be just, and if He weren't just, He would compromise His own holy character.

But what if someone else were to pay the penalty for us? God only demands that the penalty for breaking His law be meted out once. If someone else were to bear that penalty for us, we would be free from the penalty. Who can bear the penalty for me? It can't be another sinner because such a person has his or her own penalty to endure. It must be someone who is free from the penalty and who is willing to endure it in my stead.

Bliss gives us the answer in these blessed words:

Jesus hath bled, and there is remission; …

In those words, he is telling us that through His death on the cross, Jesus was taking the penalty for undeserving sinners. On the cross, He endured my eternal wrath and the eternal wrath of all who will trust in Him. There is remission—forgiveness—for sinners through the death of Christ. The cross is nothing less than this… Jesus paying the penalty for law-breakers so those law-breakers are free from the penalty. No wonder Bliss could write:

Free from the law, O happy condition.

But how could Jesus on the cross receive an eternity's worth of wrath for all sinners who believe in Him? He couldn't if He had been just another man, but He was the God-man—God in human flesh! Fully God, fully man! Since He was God, an Infinite person, Jesus could receive in a finite length of time the eternal wrath of God, He could receive it for a multitude of sinners at the same time, and He could pay the penalty "once for all." How fitting that Bliss should include as the chorus these glorious words:

Once for all, O sinner, receive it,
Once for all, O brother, believe it;
Cling to the Cross, the burden will fall,
Christ hath redeemed us once for all.

-11-

From God's Word, the Bible...

Enoch lived sixty-five years, and begot Methuselah. After he begot Methuselah, Enoch walked with God three hundred years, and had sons and daughters. So all the days of Enoch were three hundred and sixty-five years. And Enoch walked with God; and he was not, for God took him.

Genesis 5:21-24

Mr. Walking with God

When we hear the name Enoch, we immediately think of the man who was taken into heaven without having to experience death. The author of Hebrews tells us that Enoch "did not see death" but rather was "translated" into heaven (Heb. 11:5).

Immediate translation into heaven is such a sensational thing that we are apt to focus too much on it and not enough on something else. What is the something else? It is the fact that Enoch "walked with God" (vv. 22, 24). The walking with God ought to stir us as much as the matter of being translated into heaven.

It's so very easy for us to read the words of the Bible without really thinking about what we are reading. Enoch "walked with God." Think about that. We know several things about Enoch. We know he was a sinful man. He was a descendant of Adam (the seventh from Adam—Jude 14), and the sin of Adam had come upon all his descendants. We also know that Enoch was weak and limited in many ways. He was a human being, and all humans are weak and limited. Further, we know that Enoch was mortal. Even though he did not die, he was certainly subject to death.

We also know certain things about the One with whom Enoch walked, that is, God. God is eternal, holy (without sin), and unlimited in power and wisdom.

Here then is the message of the above Scripture—a sinful, limited, and mortal man walked with, that is, had close communion with, the holy, wise, powerful, and eternal God. What an amazing thing! What a privilege for Enoch!

How was such a thing possible? How was it possible for Enoch to walk with God? Amos 3:3 asks this question: "Can two walk together unless they are agreed?"

The expected answer, of course, is that they cannot. So God and Enoch had to be in agreement before they could walk together. We can be sure that God did not agree with Enoch in his sinfulness. That could never be! So Enoch had to agree with God. He had to agree that God was holy, that he, Enoch, was a sinner, and the only way for him to walk with God was to be forgiven. He further had to agree with God that there was a way for his sins to be forgiven and that was the way that God had announced in the Garden of Eden, that is, through what Christ would do.

It's interesting that Enoch began walking with God after the birth of his son Methuselah (v. 22). The name Methuselah means "When he is dead, it shall be sent." God evidently gave Enoch a revelation of what was to come, and Enoch gave testimony to that revelation by naming his son Methuselah. What was to come? The wrath of God in the form of a great flood! Enoch saw that and began to walk with God. If the coming wrath of God isn't enough to make us walk with God now, what will it take?

So Enoch began walking with God, and he kept it up until he walked body and soul into heaven itself. Enoch's experience shows us that there is a life beyond this life, and that life includes the body. God's people will eventually dwell in new bodies on a new earth. That future belongs to them, not because of any good thing they have done or will do to earn or deserve it, but rather because God has been willing to stoop down in grace and walk with them.

Let's never forget that God only walks with sinners if their sins are forgiven, and their sins can only be forgiven because of the redeeming work of Jesus. Because of what Jesus did, God walks with sinners now, and they with Him; and one blessed day they will walk right into heaven itself. When Jesus returns, Christians on earth will, like Enoch, be immediately translated into heaven (1 Thess. 4:16-17), but most Christians, unlike Enoch, will die. But it is the privilege of all Christians to walk with God.

Do you, like Enoch, endeavor to walk with God each day in the reading of His Word, the Bible, and in prayer? May He walk with you, too, as you cultivate an attitude of conscious and deliberate obedience to Him!

-12-

From God's Word, the Bible...

*So the service of the house of the LORD was set in order.
Then Hezekiah and all the people rejoiced that God had prepared
the people, since the events took place so suddenly.*

2 Chronicles 29:35-36

Two Men and Three M's

Let's call Hezekiah the 3-M man with the first M standing for mess. That's exactly what Hezekiah found when he came to the throne of the kingdom of Judah. The reason Hezekiah found a mess is because his father, Ahaz, left a mess. How did Ahaz create such a mess? Can we attribute it to unfortunate political developments that no one could have predicted? No, not at all. The mess came about because Ahaz "became increasingly unfaithful to the LORD" (28:22). He had "encouraged moral decline in Judah and had been continually unfaithful to the LORD" (28:19).

Just how bad was Ahaz? He wholeheartedly went after idols (28:23-25) and even "shut up the doors of the house of the LORD" (28:24).

Unfaithfulness to God always causes trouble, and Judah had plenty of trouble. Enemies were attacking her (28:17-18, 20-21), and many of her citizens had been killed or deported (29:9).

One statement perfectly summarizes the mess: "For the LORD brought Judah low because of Ahaz ..." (28:19).

Let the second M stand for measures. When Hezekiah became king, he saw the mess and immediately took measures. He opened the temple and cleansed and repaired it (29:3-19), brought back the temple worship (29:20-36), and restored the observance of the Passover (30:1-27).

And the third M must stand for marvel, that is, the marvel of his people rejoicing in true spiritual renewal (29:30, 36).

Here is a good summary of it: "So there was great joy in Jerusalem, for since the time of Solomon the Son of David, king of Israel, there had been nothing like this in Jerusalem" (30:26).

Our idols always promise to bring us joy, but they never do. When we leave God behind, we leave our joy behind. When we come back to God, we come back to joy.

The mess, the measures, and the marvel of Hezekiah make me think of a greater man than Hezekiah. That would be the Lord Jesus Christ, who came to a greater mess and took greater measures so He might witness a greater marvel.

The mess to which Jesus came was the mess created by sin. What a mess it was! God created everything good, but sin entered through the subtlety of Satan and the silliness of Adam and Eve. And things have never been the same. Sin has affected each and every individual since Adam (Rom. 5:12). It has darkened our minds so we can't understand the things of God. It has degraded our affections so that we don't desire the things of God. And it has deadened our wills so that we don't seek the things of God. And since each individual is affected by sin, it's inevitable that the whole world will be affected by it. The world is merely a collection of sinners. The wars, crime, hunger, political corruption, immorality, strife, hatred, and deceitfulness with which nations must cope are all due to sin.

As Hezekiah took certain measures to deal with the mess of Judah, so the Lord Jesus took measures—greater measures—to deal with the mess of sin. He, Jesus, could have stayed away from it all, but, thank God, He didn't. He became one of us, lived in perfect obedience to God, and died a special kind of death on the cross—a death in which He received the wrath that our sins deserve. He then arose from the grave, ascended to the Father in heaven, and poured out the Holy Spirit to deal with our darkness, degradedness, and deadness. Sin created a perfect mess, but the Lord provides a perfect salvation for all who trust in Him.

And that salvation will culminate in a marvel. All of the saved will finally be gathered around the Lord Jesus in eternal glory. There Jesus will see the end of the salvation that He provided for sinners, and He will rejoice. He will rejoice in seeing all of His people there, and they will rejoice in being there. But they will rejoice even more in the One who brought them there, gladly singing:

> "Blessing and honor and glory and power
> Be to Him who sits on the throne,
> And to the Lamb, forever and ever!"
> (Rev. 5:13)

-13-

From God's Word, the Bible...

Elihu also proceeded and said:
"Bear with me a little, and I will show you
That there are yet words to speak on God's behalf.
I will fetch my knowledge from afar;
I will ascribe righteousness to my Maker.
For truly my words are not false;
One who is perfect in knowledge is with you."

Job 36:1-4

Something to Be Said for God

The story of Job is well known. Although he was a righteous man, he was called to endure enormous calamities. After losing his children and his possessions, he found himself covered with painful boils. To top it all off, he was subjected to the pat answers of know-it-all friends.

All of this constituted a severe test of faith for Job, and he said some things that make us think his faith had finally snapped (Job 23:1-7; 30:20-23).

Chapter 31 ends with these words: "The words of Job are ended." And, yes, Job ended his words with a thundering defense of his own righteousness and with the unmistakable suggestion that God had failed him. He, Job, was righteous and God was unrighteous! As we look at his sufferings and read his words, we might say that Job won the argument and that there was nothing more to be said for God.

Then Elihu stepped in to tell Job that he didn't buy the notion that Job had said everything that was to be said about

God. Elihu rather insisted that there were "yet words to speak on God's behalf" (v. 2).

There's always something more to be said for God. In times of profound disillusionment and keen disappointment, it's easy for us to conclude that God has failed us. It's all very clear to us. If God were doing what He is supposed to do, our lives would be such and such. So when our lives fall short of such and such, we can pronounce God a failure. The case seems open and shut!

If Elihu could come before us, he would say the same to us as he did to Job. There is more to be said for God! What is that more? Elihu tells us: "One who is perfect in knowledge is with you" (v. 4).

So Elihu offers a breathtaking assertion—our trials come from One who is perfect in knowledge!

What does it mean to say God is perfect in knowledge? We can't give a perfect answer. The God who is perfect in knowledge far exceeds our knowledge! But we can say there are no gaps or breakdowns in His knowledge. When painful adversity comes our way, we must not allow ourselves to think that God's knowledge doesn't cover that or that it is due to God having a momentary lapse.

God's perfect knowledge extends even to our trials. He never has to say, "Oops!"

This may have come as a startling word for Job. His suffering had not come because of a failure in God's knowledge. The trials were part of God's perfect knowledge.

Standing on the back end of a life that had seen plenty of hardship, Joseph was able to say: "God meant it for good" (Gen. 50:20).

How can we be sure God is perfect in knowledge? We can look at the natural world. Such complexity, beauty, and order could only come from One who is perfect in knowledge (Ps. 19:1-8).

We can also look at the Lord Jesus dying on the cross. God's justice demanded the eternal separation of sinners from God, while God's grace pleaded for sinners to be released from that penalty. How could these seemingly contradictory demands be satisfied? How could God honor both His justice and His grace? How could he both punish guilty sinners and release them from punishment?

The perfect knowledge of God gave the answer, and the answer was Jesus. He received on the cross what justice demanded, and because He received it, all sinners who repent and believe will not receive the same. So both justice and grace were satisfied by the cross.

Elihu said something else that we must not miss. The God who was perfect in knowledge was with Job (v. 2). There were times when Job felt completely abandoned by God, but he wasn't abandoned. The God whose perfect knowledge devised the trial was with Job in the midst of it to strengthen and sustain him. And we may rest assured that the God who has promised to never leave or forsake us is with us in our trials as well (Heb. 13:5-6).

/ # -14-

From God's Word, the Bible...

Moreover, because I have set my affection on the house of my God, I have given to the house of my God, over and above all that I have prepared for the holy house, my own special treasure of gold and silver.

1 Chronicles 29:3

Good Things from a Good Man

This verse is part of the wrapping up phase of David's life. He was wrapping up both his forty-year reign over Israel and his life. He had two major things on his mind—the success of his son and successor, Solomon, and the building of the temple. While the Lord didn't allow David to build it (1 Chron. 22:8; 28:3), He did allow him to gather materials for its construction. And gather materials David did! David records: "Now for the house of my God, I have prepared with all my might ..." (v. 2).

So what are the good things that David gives us in this verse? The first is *a good choice*.

There were all kinds of things calling for David's affection—many of which were legitimate—but he had made a choice. He would not set his affection on lesser things. He would set it on God and His house.

David knew if he didn't control his affections, they would control him. We must understand that there are some things that we should not love at all, and there are some things that we should love a lot less than we do, and we must take charge of our affections or they will carry us away.

The reason so many churches are in decline is this: most church members can't say what David said. They haven't set their affection on the house of God.

Yes, society has changed drastically. There is no longer a general attitude of friendliness toward the church. But the main problem in our churches is not the attitude of the world. It is the attitude of church members who essentially say: "We will not make the church our priority. We will put anything and everything above the church, and whatever we have left, we will give to the church."

The second good thing David gives us is *the good reason for his good choice.*

Why did David love the house of God to the extent that he put it over other things? The answer is in the words—"my God." David loved the house of God because God had become his God.

How does God become our God? This doesn't happen automatically. Our sin, which separates us from God, has to be taken out of the way, and the only way sin can be taken out of the way is for its penalty to be paid.

The temple on which David had set his affection would be the place of atonement. The high priest of Israel would enter one time each year into THE MOST HOLY PLACE to sprinkle the blood of a sacrifice on the mercy seat—and that pictured and anticipated what Jesus would do for sinners on the cross.

By the way, we would do well to hear Jesus speaking words similar to those of David. Before the world began, the Lord Jesus said to the Father: "I have set My affection on the church and will go to the earth and die for her." This is clear from the words of the Apostle Paul in Ephesians 5:25-27.

The Lord Jesus has done everything necessary for us to be saved from our sins, to be reconciled to God, and made part of His church. He now calls us to put our trust in Him and in what He has done (Acts 16:30).

Finally, David gives us *the good result of his good choice*.

David's good choice led him to act. In addition to collecting materials for the temple, David gave his "special treasure of gold and silver."

We have the tendency to restrict love for God and His house to a feeling. We think it's possible to love God and His house without doing anything. We wouldn't think of using that logic in any other area of life. We would never say, "I love football, but I never take any action. I never watch a game on TV or go to a game."

If we heard someone say that, we would respond by saying, "You don't really love football. You just think you do."

So it is with the matter of loving the Lord. If we say we love God and never do anything to show it, we don't really love Him at all. We just think we do.

Are you showing by your life and actions that you love the Lord and are committed to serving Him in all ways you are able?

-15-

From God's Word, the Bible...

By faith Abel offered to God a more excellent sacrifice than Cain, through which he obtained witness that he was righteous, God testifying of his gifts; and through it he being dead still speaks.

Hebrews 11:4

(Please also read Genesis 4:1-8)

Mr. First in Heaven

While Adam was the first man on earth, he was not the first man to make it to heaven. That distinction goes to his second son. Abel was the first man to die, but he didn't go to heaven because he died. Salvation by death is perhaps the most widely held belief of our day, but it is mistaken. Merely dying doesn't qualify anyone to enter heaven.

Abel went to heaven because of his faith in the coming Christ. God has always had one and only one plan of salvation for sinners, and that plan is His Son, Jesus Christ. People in the Old Testament era were saved as they looked forward in faith to the Christ who was to come. After Christ came, people are saved as they look backward in faith to Him. We should get rid of the notion that God tried one plan of salvation for a while, ditched it, tried another, ditched it, and so on. God's plan has always been Christ.

To say Abel is in heaven today is to say he looked forward in faith to the redeeming work of Christ. This is indicated by his offering. He brought to God an offering that shed blood. Where did he get that idea? His parents undoubtedly told him about God picturing the coming Christ by shedding the blood of animals (Gen. 3:21). Abel heard that, believed it, and acted upon it. What is faith? It is believing the Word of God.

Cain heard the same truths, but refused to believe. He recreated his parents' fig-leaf aprons (Gen. 3:7) by bringing to God the works of his own hands. God was no more pleased with that than He was with the aprons. So He rejected Cain's offering and accepted Abel's.

Enraged, Cain killed his brother. He couldn't kill God, so he did the next best thing. We're still seeing it today. People who hate God and would like to kill Him have to settle instead for persecuting His people.

There was more to Abel than his physical body. Like all of us, he was body and soul. We do not know what happened to his body. We assume that Adam and Eve buried it in the ground or sealed it in a cave. But we know what happened to his soul. It went to be with God in heaven. How do we know this to be true? The Bible makes it plain (Eccl.12:7-8; Luke 23:43; 2 Cor. 5:1-8).

So Abel's soul went to heaven on the day that he died, and it has been there ever since. Abel has been in heaven longer than anyone else.

That doesn't mean there is no future for Abel's body. That body, long since turned to dust, will rise again. The Bible tells us that the Lord Jesus will come again with the souls of all those believers who have died (1 Thess. 4:14), will raise their bodies from their graves, and reunite their souls with their bodies. But it will not be so they can resume life on this earth as they knew it before, but rather so they can enter into the glorious resurrection life that the Lord Jesus Himself now has—and that will be glorious resurrection life in a new heaven and on a new earth!

How is it possible for a body that has completely turned

to dust to be raised? The God who had the power to make the first man from the dust (Gen. 2:7) can surely raise one from the dust!

So Cain killed Abel, and Abel went to heaven. Years later, Cain himself died, but he did not go to heaven (1 John 3:10-15). What was the difference between Cain and Abel? The author of Hebrews answers in two words: "by faith" (Heb. 11:4).

Abel had the faith and went to heaven. Cain did not have it and did not go to heaven. With Cain and Abel, the whole human race was divided into two streams. One stream is Cain's, which is rejecting God's revealed plan of salvation. The other is Abel's, which is accepting that plan.

If you have true and saving faith in Christ, you, like Abel, will go to heaven—not because of any good works that you ever did or could do, but only because of God's love and saving grace shown to you!

-16-

From God's Word, the Bible...

And when he had found him, he brought him to Antioch. So it was that for a whole year they assembled with the church and taught a great many people. And the disciples were first called Christians in Antioch.

Acts 11:26

Just Call Me a Christian

I have followed major league baseball since my childhood years. I find the nicknames for various players to be one of the more fascinating elements of the game.

Some of my favorites are: High Pockets Kelly (the man was so tall that his pockets were higher than those of anyone else), No-Neck Williams (whose head appeared to sit directly on his shoulders with nothing between), Three Finger Brown (who had lost parts of two fingers on his pitching hand), Bucketfoot Al (because of the exaggerated step he took toward third base when he was hitting), Bonehead Merkle (given because of a particularly egregious base-running blunder) and Old Tomato Face (you'll have to figure that one out for yourself).

In Acts 11:26, Luke, the author of Acts, notes the nickname that was given to followers of the Lord Jesus Christ in the early days of the New Testament church. That name was "Christians." The name means "Christ ones" or "Christ people." It referred to those who believed in Christ, loved Him, followed Him, and served Him.

Was this nickname given out of hatred and contempt or, as the commentator John Stott suggests, in a "familiar and jocular" way? Was it a lighthearted joke or a mean-spirited jab? We don't know. Whatever it was, the disciples of those days liked it so much that they began to use it themselves.

Maybe the question is not so much what unbelievers think about the name "Christian," but rather what we Christians should think about it. The name should remind us that Christ is the center, the focal point, the very sum and substance of Christianity. There is no Christianity without Him. Therefore, we should heartily resist the temptation to turn Christianity into nothing more than a life management technique, that is, a way to cope with life's problems and to manage its demands. While Christianity does help us face the challenges of life, that is secondary. We should let the name "Christian" remind us of what we owe the Lord Jesus. That is the main thing. We owe a debt that we cannot pay because Jesus paid a debt that He did not owe. On the cross, Jesus paid the penalty for our sins so we do not have to pay that penalty ourselves.

Those who know nothing about the reality of their sins and about the enormity of having to stand before a holy God in those sins can't possibly understand Christians. They will always be befuddled when they hear us sing:

> *In Christ alone my hope is found;*
> *He is my light, my strength, my song ...*

But Christians, knowing the awesome weight of sin and judgment, will not be deterred by the unknowing world but will hurry on to add:

> *In Christ alone, who took on flesh,*
> *Fullness of God in helpless babe!*
> *This gift of love and righteousness,*
> *Scorned by the ones He came to save.*
> *Till on that cross as Jesus died,*
> *The wrath of God was satisfied;*
> *For ev'ry sin on Him was laid—*
> *Here in the death of Christ I live*
> (Keith Getty and Stuart Townend)

We should also let the word "Christian" constantly challenge us to live in such way that those around us will know that Christ is the main part and the best part of our lives. We should live in such a way that others will know that we are Christians before we are anything else—Christians in our speech, our thoughts, our conduct, our attitudes, our goals, our homes.

Our Christianity should so fill us and thrill us that we eagerly join the martyr Polycarp in saying: "Hear me declare with boldness, I am a Christian."

Or we can put it in the words of Baynard L. Fox:

> *I'll tell the world that I'm a Christian,*
> *I'm not ashamed His name to bear;*
> *I'll tell the world that I'm a Christian,*
> *I'll take Him with me anywhere.*
>
> ...
>
> *I'll tell the world that He's my Savior,*
> *No other one could love me so;*
> *My life, my all is His forever,*
> *And where He leads me I will go.*

-17-

From God's Word, the Bible...

I went by the field of the lazy man,
And by the vineyard of the man devoid of understanding;
And there it was, all overgrown with thorns;
Its surface was covered with nettles;
Its stone wall was broken down.
When I saw it, I considered it well;
I looked on it and received instruction:
A little sleep, a little slumber,
A little folding of the hands to rest;
So shall your poverty come like a prowler,
And your need like an armed man.

Proverbs 24:30-34

The Sluggard's Garden

Out for his morning walk, King Solomon, the author of Proverbs, came upon a sad sight. It was a neglected garden. Thorns and nettles were everywhere, and the protecting wall was broken down.

From his vantage point, Solomon may have been able to look through the window of the house and see the gardener (or non-gardener). Lying in his recliner, he stirs, looks briefly out the window at his garden, folds his hands, and goes back to sleep.

Perhaps he was sick and unable to work. But no, that wasn't the case. This man, probably well known in the community, was lazy—a sluggard. There he is at the coffee shop. The talk turns to gardens and vineyards. One man relates his plans for improving his yield, and another man does the same. Our lazy friend chimes in: he also has great plans for his garden, but he's no sooner home than his resolve fades. He will tackle his garden later. Right now, he feels very tired. He will rest today, get up early tomorrow, and set to work. He will be able to do much more work tomorrow if he gets enough rest today.

So he goes to his easy chair. Other gardeners are hard at work with watering, pruning and weeding—but not the sluggard.

Lazy? Yes! But Solomon tells us that this man's laziness was merely the manifestation of another problem. This man was "devoid of understanding" (v. 30). He was stupid. He didn't realize that his own happiness and wellbeing were tied to that garden. If it didn't produce, he would have no goods to sell and nothing to eat. His negligence was tantamount to allowing a burglar to come into his home to carry off his valuables (v. 34). That neglected garden and the burglar would have the same effect on this lazy man. Each would deprive him of those things he needed to live. The irony is that while this lazy man wouldn't have allowed a burglar to take his goods, he had no qualms about his untended garden.

Solomon didn't merely pass by. He stood for a while looking at the woeful garden. He "considered it well" and "received instruction" (v. 32). There was an important lesson to be learned—if we want to enjoy the fruits of vigorous labor, we must be willing to do the vigorous labor.

We would do well to learn from Solomon. There are areas of life that demand our diligent attention. If we refuse to give them that attention, we deprive ourselves of good.

Our homes require such attention. The happy home is one that is constantly weeded and guarded. The tender plants of kindness, understanding, forgiveness, and faithfulness make the home thrive, but those plants can be choked by the thorns of irritability, selfishness, bitterness, and strife. How sad it is that so many homes these days are sluggards' gardens!

Our churches require constant care and vigilance. The vile weed of gossip, the hurtful thorn of indifference, the nettle of prayerlessness, and the bramble of coldness toward the Lord and His gospel can easily pop up to choke the life out of the church.

And we as individuals would do well to consider ourselves as gardens that require diligent effort. The Bible gives us clear teaching on tending ourselves. It first urges each of us to be diligent about receiving salvation from the Lord (Luke 13:24; John 6:27). We must not allow anything to take priority over the matter of the salvation of our souls.

After we are saved, we must carefully guard or keep our hearts (Prov. 4:23). The keeping of the heart means keeping harmful things away from it and helpful things near it. We're to keep our minds from false teachings, our affections from what is base and impure, and our wills from making evil choices. And we are to keep our hearts close to the Word of God. Keeping close to the Word of God means reading it regularly, carefully, reverently, and prayerfully. It also involves faithfully going to the house of God where the Word of God is proclaimed.

Of this we can be sure—the devil is not a sluggard. He is busily at work to destroy our homes, our churches, and our souls. If we are sluggards in these areas, he will succeed.

-18-

From God's Word, the Bible...

Can flavorless food be eaten without salt?
Or is there any taste in the white of an egg?

Job 6:6

Dining on the White of an Egg

Is anything more tasteless, more bland, more unappetizing than an unsalted egg white? So when Job asks if there is any taste in the white of an egg, we're ready with the resounding answer—No!

Job raised the question to defend his bitter complaining about his suffering. By raising a series of questions, Job was insisting that he had a perfect right to complain. Does a wild donkey bray when it has grass? Of course not. Does an ox low if it has fodder? No. Can flavorless food be eaten without salt? Hardly. Is there any taste in the white of an egg? None.

Job was essentially asking this question: "Would I be complaining if I had no legitimate reason?" And his friends would have to answer in exactly the same way as they would with his other questions: "No, Job, you wouldn't complain unless there was a good reason."

As far as Job was concerned, his life had been reduced to

the tasteless white of an egg, and he was entitled to complain about it.

It occurs to me that each day of our lives is something like pulling up to the table to eat a meal. Some days we have very tasty morsels and delicacies set before us, and we are delighted. It's easy to be thankful on such days.

On other days we have common but satisfying fare. These are the meat-and-potato days, and while we aren't exhilarated by these things, we eat and are satisfied. This is the routine part of life, and most of us have to work a bit to be truly thankful for it.

Then there are those days when the only thing we find on the plate of life is the white of an egg, and it seems that there is not so much as a single grain of salt in the saltshaker. So we eat and say, "Ugh," and we may very well think we have no obligation to be thankful at all.

These are the days in which our circumstances run against us, and the joy of living evaporates before our eyes. Serious illness, the death of a loved one, financial reversal, the rebellion of a child, the fracture of a friendship, the steady deterioration of society—all of these things and more can constitute a meal of egg whites. No salt; no ketchup; no pepper—just a tasteless, loathsome portion that we must eat! We stare at it, and it stares at us, and we wonder how we are going to be able to choke it down.

We always want God to explain why we have egg whites on our plates. Job never received the full explanation that he wanted. The book ends with Job realizing that God owes no one an explanation for what He does in his or her life. While Job didn't get his explanation, it was enough for him to know that God had the explanation.

We may not understand our difficulties in this life. If that's the case, let's try to content ourselves with knowing that God knows the reasons for them and will eventually make them plain. We'll understand it better by and by.

And let's remember when we have egg whites on our plates, that there is always some salt there as well. It may seem that there is no salt at all, but a closer look will reveal that there is.

In other words, the Christian always has resources for facing the trials of life—the Word of God, the house of God, prayer.

Remember this as well: a day is coming when egg whites will be forever removed from the menu for the children of God. In heaven we will dine on the delicacies that God has reserved for those who know Him and love Him. Let's never forget that we know and love God because of the redeeming work of the Lord Jesus Christ. No matter how severe their trials, Christians always have reason to be thankful to God, and the greatest of those reasons is the Lord Jesus.

.

-19-

From God's Word, the Bible...

All you beasts of the field, come to devour,
All you beasts in the forest.
His watchmen are blind, They are all ignorant;
They are all dumb dogs, They cannot bark;
Sleeping, lying down, loving to slumber.
Yes, they are greedy dogs which never have enough.
And they are shepherds who cannot understand;
They all look to their own way,
Every one for his own gain,
From his own territory.
"Come," one says, "I will bring wine,
And we will fill ourselves with intoxicating drink;
Tomorrow will be as today, and much more abundant."

Isaiah 56:9-12

Dogs That Won't Bark

Sometimes I think my wife and I should have bought a Basenji. What is a Basenji? It is a dog without a bark.

The reason I think that from time to time is that our dog Molly barks and barks and barks. A good bit of her day is taken up with barking. She barks at people who are taking their walks (and especially if they happen to be walking their dogs). She barks at delivery people. She barks at the mail truck. She barks at neighbors who are working in their yards. She barks when someone knocks or rings the doorbell. She has a special hatred for the boxer (a dog, not a fighter) that lives next door, and barks furiously every time she sees him.

Molly loves to bark, and it can get rather annoying because she has a very loud bark. She is the little dog with the big bark.

Annoying? Yes. But I recognize that there may come a time when Molly's bark has real value. If a burglar were to attempt to sneak in while we are sleeping, Molly would most certainly hear him and sound the alarm. What good is a dog without a bark when a danger is threatening the family?

The people of Judah were facing real danger: "beasts of the field" were coming "to devour" (v. 9). The crying need was for the "watchmen" stationed on the wall of the city to see the danger and sound the alarm, but, alas, the watchmen were "dumb dogs" that "cannot bark." They preferred to lie down and take a nap rather than exert the energy to bark (v. 10).

All of this constitutes a picture of a far greater reality. Judah wasn't being threatened by literal beasts. She was rather being threatened by foreign nations who hated her and wanted to destroy her. And the term "watchmen" doesn't really refer to the men on the wall. It rather refers to the spiritual leaders of the nation who should have had enough discernment to see the situation. They should have seen that Judah's enemies were coming against her because of the sinfulness of the people, and they should have called them to repent.

We need Mollys in our pulpits today. We need preachers who will bark at the sight of danger. We need men who will tell sinners that they are sinners, and if they don't flee to Christ in true repentance and faith they are facing "everlasting destruction" (2 Thess. 1:9).

We need preachers who will warn Christians that spiritual coldness and indifference will lead to woeful results for themselves as individuals and for the church in general.

The sad truth is many preachers won't bark. They have opted for a "feel-good" religion.

Why is it that so many preachers refuse to bark these days? Many are more concerned about the times than they are about the truth. They read opinion polls with more interest and fervor than they read the Word of God. They dread nothing more than being out of step.

Then there are those who tone down the message out of their concern for "nickels and noses." They don't want to run the risk of offending their hearers because they want to keep them coming to church and want them to continue giving their money.

A non-barking preacher is dangerous and should be avoided, but a barking preacher is an inestimable treasure. If you don't have a barking preacher, find one, and if you do have one, pray for him and prize him. Someone has observed that the pastor who loves his people the most is the one who tells them the most truth about themselves.

I'm thankful that many years ago, a common, ordinary preacher stepped into the pulpit and barked at me. He told me that I must leave this world and stand before a holy God. He told me about my sin, and, thank God, he told me that God forgives sinners on the basis of the redeeming work of Christ. When I meet that preacher in heaven, I want to weep, fall on his neck, and kiss him (Acts 20:37).

Thank God for a barking preacher.

-20-

From God's Word, the Bible...

And the kings of the earth, the great men, the rich men, the commanders, the mighty men, every slave and every free man, hid themselves in the caves and in the rocks of the mountains, and said to the mountains and rocks, "Fall on us and hide us from the face of Him who sits on the throne and from the wrath of the Lamb! For the great day of His wrath has come, and who is able to stand?"

Revelation 6:15-17

The Day the Prayer-Shamers Will Pray

Shaming has become a thriving business. There is gender-shaming, fat-shaming (or body-shaming), race-shaming, and ugly-shaming. There's even shame-shaming, that is, shaming people for heaping shame on others.

Now we can add prayer-shaming to the list. This came to light shortly after a deranged, angry man walked into a Texas church on November 5, 2017, and killed twenty-six people.

People all across the nation responded by telling us that we should pray for the families of the victims, and immediately the prayer-shamers came out. Actors and actresses, political leaders, journalists, and members of academe joined the chorus of scorn on the call for prayer. Some observed that the victims of this massacre were in a church and part of what they were doing there was praying. So, they reasoned, if prayer does any good, these people wouldn't have been killed.

It should be observed that these same people would never shame Muslims or people of other faiths for praying. But Christians are always fair game for the shaming industry.

So it set me to thinking about prayer. How much the Bible makes of it! Someone has calculated that there are 650 prayers recorded in the Bible. That's a lot! In addition to the actual prayers, there is much teaching about the matter. For example we are told to pray without ceasing (1 Thess. 5:17). That doesn't mean we should never do anything except pray, but rather that we should be constantly resorting to prayer. The Christian should never be far from prayer.

But there is a misconception about prayer. The prayer-shamers seem to think that every prayer a Christian offers has to be answered in the way that the Christian wants, or all of his Christianity must come crashing down on his head. Let one prayer seem to fail, and all of Christianity fails, they say!

But nowhere does the Bible tell us that prayer is the way of getting our will done in heaven. It is one way that God has appointed for getting His will done on earth.

By the way, Christians have been praying for centuries and centuries, and, yes, all through those centuries there have been all kinds of tragedies. Prayer doesn't inoculate us from tragedy; it rather gives us strength in the midst of it.

Where do all these tragedies come from? The Bible that makes so much of prayer gives us the answer. Sin is the cause of all the heartaches, all the sorrow, and all the pain in this world. But it's much easier to be a prayer-shamer than a sin-shamer. We always want to blame God for the results of our sin. That has been going on since the Garden of Eden (Gen. 3:12) and will continue till the end of time. But God has consistently warned us about the terrible consequences of sin, and urged us to be done with it. It wasn't God that caused the Texas tragedy—it was a sinner. Could God have prevented it? Yes, but God usually chooses to put the consequences of horrible sin on full display so we will get sick of it and turn from it

The prayer-shaming that took place after the Texas massacre also made me think of a day when the prayer-shamers themselves will pray. It is recorded for us in these words:

> And the kings of the earth, the great men, the rich men, the commanders, the mighty men, every slave and every free man, hid themselves in the caves and in the rocks of the mountains, and said to the mountains and rocks, "Fall on us and hide us from the face of Him who sits on the throne and from the wrath of the Lamb! For the great day of His wrath has come, and who is able to stand?" (Rev. 6:15-17).

But that prayer will have the wrong address (to the mountains instead of to God) and for the wrong thing (to escape from God). And it will be too late.

It comes down to this: we can pray now to draw near to God or we can pray then to get away from Him. God has made a way for sinful people to come to Him in a personal relationship through His Son—by turning away from sin, and by trusting in Him as their Redeemer. Of this we may be sure: we will all be pray-ers in one way or another.

.

-21-

From God's Word, the Bible...

Do not be deceived, God is not mocked; for whatever a man sows, that he will also reap. For he who sows to his flesh will of the flesh reap corruption, but he who sows to the Spirit will of the Spirit reap everlasting life. And let us not grow weary while doing good, for in due season we shall reap if we do not lose heart.

Galatians 6:7-9

Sowing and Reaping

It was late, and I had just gone to bed. The phone rang. "This is Bob. I heard you preach last Sunday morning, and I'm hoping you can help me."

I asked Bob to come to my study the next morning. His problem was alcohol. He told me that his boss was going to fire him, and his wife was going to leave him if he didn't stop drinking. His doctor had also told him that he was wrecking his health by his drinking.

Here was his question: "What should I do?"

I found myself wondering whether counseling could really be this easy. . .

Then I said to Bob: "I think I have the answer for you."

"What's that?" he eagerly asked.

I replied: "Stop drinking!"

Would you like to guess what his answer was? He said: "Oh, I could never do that."

In my early years as a pastor, I was often frustrated by my attempts to provide counseling for people. It seemed to me that the counseling rarely did any good. People would come with a problem, I would counsel, and nothing would change. The problem would persist.

I would blame myself, thinking if I were a better counselor I would have more success in making problems go away. So I bought several books on counseling and read them, hoping that I could find the "secret" to being a better counselor.

My experience with Bob gave me new insight on the matter of counseling. After talking with him, I realized that I had been trying to change my counselees' reaping when they were not willing to change their sowing.

In other words, I was trying to do what no counselor on earth can do. No counselor can change what people reap if they are not willing to change what they sow.

Bob wanted me to change his reaping. He wanted me to take away the terrible consequences of his drinking, but he was not willing to stop doing the very thing that was producing those consequences.

My mother prominently posted *The Prayer of Serenity* in our home. So I saw if often as I was growing up:

> *God, grant me the serenity to accept the things I cannot change;*
> *Courage to change the things I can,*
> *and wisdom to know the difference.*

There's a lot of wisdom in that prayer. The sad truth is that many people try to change things that simply cannot be changed and refuse to change those things that can and should be changed.

We can't change the fact that we are all sowing a crop, and we are going to reap exactly what we sow. No farmer sows soybeans so that he can reap corn. If he wants corn, he has to plant corn. God has put the law of sowing and reaping in place, and for us to think we can change it is to essentially mock God (v. 7).

But there are things that can be changed. We can change where we sow. Paul says we can sow in the flesh or in the Spirit. Over here is the field of the flesh. Over there is the field of the Spirit. Which field are you sowing in? If you are in the field of the flesh, you should change fields. Get in the realm of the Spirit of God by repenting of your sins and trusting in the Lord Jesus Christ and in what He did for sinners (Rom. 8:1-2).

Once we get in the field of the Spirit, we can change how much we sow in the spiritual realm. As Christians, we can sow bountifully or sparingly. If we sow bountifully in spiritual things, we will reap bountifully. If we sow sparingly, we will reap sparingly (2 Cor. 9:6).

And we can change how consistently we sow in the spiritual realm. Some sow for a while, and get discouraged. So Paul tells us not to get weary in well doing (v. 9), and the author of Ecclesiastes says:

> *In the morning sow your seed,*
> *And in the evening do not*
> *withhold your hand …*
> (Eccl. 11:6).

I don't know what became of Bob, but I do know this—God's law of sowing and reaping has not changed. We must not deny it, but we must sow wisely.

-22-

From God's Word, the Bible...

For now we see in a mirror, dimly, but then face to face. Now I know in part, but then I shall know just as I also am known.

1 Corinthians 13:12

Moms and Mysteries

My wife and I were immeasurably blessed with godly mothers. My wife's mother died very suddenly on the morning of September 29, 1978. She was fifty-five years old and seemingly in good health. Such a wonderful person so quickly removed!

My mother, on the hand, died on March 29, 1992, after spending her last years in a nursing home. It was a long visit, eight years, from an unwelcome guest, Parkinson's disease.

During those years, I would visit as often as I could. It was a very difficult thing. As the disease ravaged her body, she got to the place where she was unable to do even the simplest things. She couldn't adjust her glasses, operate the TV remote, feed herself or pick up her Bible. All she could do was lie there. And her speech became so garbled that listening to her was primarily guesswork. It was a matter of trying to understand a couple of words here and there and guessing about the rest of her words. It was such a heartbreaking thing that I would always leave in tears.

I think you will understand when I say I was relieved when the Lord finally took her home.

During those eight years, my mother, who had taught me so much, continued to teach me.

One of those things was *the importance of smiling through hardship*. While Mr. Parkinson assaulted her body, he could not touch her spirit. She had smiled her way through many hardships, and she continued to smile till the end.

She also taught me *the importance of giving priority to prayer*.

I would sometimes say to her: "Mom, I'm so sorry that you are going through all of this. I'm sorry you can't do any of the things you used to enjoy so much."

And she would always smile and say: "I can still pray."

Then there *was the importance of continuing to love and trust the Lord.* We are called to trust the Lord when our circumstances are good and when they are not so good, when life is like a light summer breeze and when it is like the blowing of a fierce gale.

I would say that my mother never lost her faith, but I realize that faith wasn't hers to keep. It was given to her by the Lord, and He kept her in it. He is the author and finisher of our faith (Heb. 12:2).

My mom continued to love and trust God because she understood how much the Lord loved her. She rejoiced in these words from the Apostle Paul: "Thanks be to God for His indescribable gift" (2 Cor. 9:15).

That gift, of course, is the Lord Jesus Christ through whom we can have forgiveness for our sins and eternal life.

No matter how great his burdens, the Christian can always say: "Yes, but I have the greatest of all blessings—salvation through Christ."

So there you have it—one mom cut off very suddenly in the midst of her usefulness and the other mom lingering long after most all of her usefulness was gone. In our moms, my wife and I came face to face with mystery.

Some would tell us that each of these two cases is reason to turn against God. But how can we turn against the One who gave us our moms and, more importantly, gave us the Lord Jesus?

As I've said many times: I don't trust God because He gives me the answers to all my questions. I trust Him because He has given me answers I cannot get around.

Our mothers now rest in the presence of the Lord, and my wife and I rest in the promises of the Lord. We rest in the words of one of those hymns my mom used to sing:

> *Trials dark on every hand,*
> *And we cannot understand,*
> *All the ways that God would lead us*
> *To that blessed Promised Land;*
> *But He'll guide us with His eye,*
> *And we'll follow till we die;*
> *We will understand it better by and by.*
> (Charles A. Tindley)

And to that, dear brother Tindley, I say: "Thank you and amen!"

-23-

From God's Word, the Bible...

Finally, my brethren, be strong in the Lord and in the power of His might. Put on the whole armor of God, that you may be able to stand against the wiles of the devil. For we do not wrestle against flesh and blood, but against principalities, against powers, against the rulers of the darkness of this age, against spiritual hosts of wickedness in the heavenly places. Therefore take up the whole armor of God, that you may be able to withstand in the evil day, and having done all, to stand.

Ephesians 6:10-13

The Song of the Severed Arm

It was on Tuesday, March 30, 1858, when five thousand men gathered in Philadelphia to hear Dudley Tyng preach. Feeling a heavy burden to see husbands and fathers come to Christ, Dudley had organized and promoted this rally.

As he stood to preach that day, Dudley felt the enormous weight of his responsibility. Preaching to five thousand eternity-bound men! He chose these words as the text for his sermon: "Go now, you who are men, and serve the Lord" (Exod. 10:11).

In his sermon, Dudley said: "I would rather this right arm were amputated at the trunk than that I should come short of my duty to you in preaching God's message."

Preach God's message he did, and over one thousand of those men professed faith in Christ that very day. But he still lost his arm!

Two weeks later, Dudley was watching a corn-thrasher.

In a careless moment, he got too close to the machine. In the blink of an eye, the machine snagged his sleeve and pulled his arm into its cogs. The arm was horribly mangled and almost completely pulled off. Infection began to set in, and what remained of the arm was amputated four days later. It soon became clear that Dudley would not survive. When he was told of his soon-coming death, Dudley responded: "Then it is very well. God's will be done." And he urged his doctor to receive the Lord Jesus Christ.

He died at age 33 on April 19, 1858. Shortly before he died, he said to some of his friends: "Let us all stand for Jesus." He also said to his father: "Stand up for Jesus, Father, and tell my brethren of the ministry, wherever you meet them, to stand up for Jesus!"

On the Sunday following Dudley's funeral, George Duffield, Jr., Pastor of Temple Presbyterian Church in Philadelphia, preached in honor of his friend from this text: "Stand, therefore, having girded your waist with truth, having put on the breastplate of righteousness" (Eph. 6:14). He closed his sermon by reading the six verses of the poem he had written. The poem began:

> *Stand up, stand up for Jesus,*
> *Ye soldiers of the cross;*
> *Lift high His royal banner,*
> *It must not suffer loss.*

The organist-composer George Webb later set the poem to music.

So Dudley Tyng's severed arm was used by God to inspire George Duffield, and Duffield's poem was used by God to inspire millions in the form of the hymn *Stand Up, Stand Up for Jesus*.

Dudley Tyng could have come down to death's door

with bitterness and anger, saying: "I have tried to faithfully serve the Lord, and here I am dying at a young age. Why is the Lord letting this happen to me?"

But there was no trace of any such thing. We might say Dudley stood for the Lord in death just as he had stood for Him in life, and he urged all around him to stand for Jesus as well.

It will be a fascinating thing to meet Dudley in heaven and talk to him about his last days on earth. I want to ask him why he continued to stand for Jesus in those days and urged others to continue to stand for Jesus. I would like to know why this matter of standing for Jesus was so much on his mind as his life ebbed away. I won't be surprised if he responds: "Jesus stood for me when He died on the cross. Why shouldn't I stand for Him?"

Dudley Tyng's death was filled with excruciating agony and pain. Even so, it couldn't begin to compare to the death of Jesus. His death was more than physical in nature. He actually received God's wrath so all who believe in Him will never have to experience it. I think Dudley would have been willing to die the same death twice to express gratitude for Jesus dying once.

Jesus' death opened heaven's doors to sinners, and heaven will be so glorious that it will make the suffering of this life seem small.

To him that overcometh,
A crown of life shall be;
He with the King of Glory
Shall reign eternally.

-24-

From God's Word, the Bible...

Rejoice in the Lord always. Again I will say, rejoice!

Philippians 4:4

The Joyful Journey

The Christian life is a journey. It begins when God visits the sinner in saving grace, and it lasts until that saved sinner leaves this world and enters heaven.

It is always a challenging journey and often a very difficult one. But while we don't marginalize or minimize the difficulties, we are to journey with joy. The Bible uses the words "joy" and "joyful" a total of 250 times. It uses the word "rejoice" 200 times. So the Bible commends a cheerful spirit at least 450 times. It is no wonder that C.S. Lewis wrote: "Joy is the serious business of heaven."

Some may wonder if it is right for us to be joyful. We see so much heartache and trouble that we might be inclined to think that we should go through life with a heavy and melancholy spirit. While the Bible does not tell us to ignore the burdens of life, it does urge us to be joyful in the midst of them.

But what should we do when we feel that our joy is slipping and sliding away from us? I propose the 3D treatment. Think about three words, each beginning with the letter D, and see if that thinking doesn't bring joy flooding in once again.

The first D stands for Departure. When your joy is fading, think about your departure.

Every Christian was once not a Christian. We all come into this world as sinners. John Bunyan's wonderful book, *The Pilgrim's Progress*, begins with the pilgrim living in the City of Destruction where he was born.

We're all born into that city. We are all sinners by nature, and, as such, we are under a sentence of destruction from the holy God.

To be a Christian means that one has come out of that city. That person has departed from it by the grace of God. Every Christian has been enlightened and enabled by that grace, that is, made to see the truth about himself or herself and enabled to lay hold of the saving work of the Lord Jesus. Every Christian can say: "I used to live in that city, but no longer. I have been brought out. I've been delivered from destruction because of what Jesus did for sinners like me."

No matter how sour your circumstances, that is enough to set your heart singing.

The second D stands for Disposition. No, I'm not talking about your attitude or frame of mind. Rather, I'm referring to how God has disposed or arranged things for His people. In other words, God has given Christians wonderful resources for their journey. They have the Spirit of God to help them (John 14:16-17), the Word of God to guide them (Ps. 119:105), the throne of God that they can approach in prayer (Heb. 4:16-18), and the people of God to encourage, strengthen, and sustain them (Phil. 1:3-5).

The journey is not joyful because of the absence of difficulties but rather because of the presence of God's supplies. If our joy is diminished, it isn't because we lack these supplies but rather because we aren't using them as well as we should.

The third D stands for Destination. I love the story of the little boy who was trying to pick out a puppy. As he carefully surveyed the litter, one puppy began wagging its tail. The boy said to his father, "I want the one with the happy ending."

What a happy ending Christians have! An eternal home in heaven! That's our destination! And that eternal home is not up in the sky somewhere. It is on a new earth. More specifically, it is on this earth after it is freed from the ravages of sin, completely cleansed and renewed (Rom. 8:19-22; 2 Peter 3:10-13; Rev. 21:1-22:5). That new earth will have one city, "the holy city, [the] New Jerusalem," (Rev. 21:2).

When we arrive in that city, we will marvel at the distance we traveled—all the way from the City of Destruction to the heavenly city.

We're not there yet, but we look forward to it, our happy ending. Thank God, we don't have to come to the end to be happy. We can—and should—be happy now.

-25-

From God's Word, the Bible...

You will keep him in perfect peace,
Whose mind is stayed on You, Because he trusts in You.
Isaiah 26:3

For thus says the LORD:
"Behold, I will extend peace to her like a river,
And the glory of the Gentiles like a flowing stream.
Then you shall feed;
On her sides shall you be carried,
And be dandled on her knees."
Isaiah 66:12

…and the peace of God, which surpasses all understanding, will guard your hearts and minds through Christ Jesus.
Philippians 4:7

The Precious Last Word

"He —!" It was the last word Frances Havergal said, or rather, sang. Her family said she started to sing, but that one word, sung with a high note, is all she was able to get out. To whom did that last "he" refer? Her family knew. It was the Lord Jesus Christ, the One she loved so very much. A little earlier, she had said: "Come, Lord Jesus, come and fetch me."

The Lord heard that prayer and took Frances home that day. She died on June 3, 1879, at age forty-two.

Every Christian loves the Lord. There can be no doubt about that. Tell me that you don't love the Lord, and I will be quick to tell you that you aren't a Christian. But there are degrees of love, and Frances Havergal loved the Lord to a high degree. It was not surprising that she was thinking about Him when she died.

Born December 14, 1836, to an Anglican pastor and his wife, Frances was a poet and hymn-writer. *Take My Life and*

Let it Be and *I Gave My Life for Thee* are two of her better-known hymns, but my favorite of all her hymns is *Like a River Glorious.*

That hymn, based on the Scriptures above, rejoices in the peace God has promised to give His people. It is perfect peace.

Frances knew and reflected this perfect peace on more than one occasion. In 1876, she got so very sick with a cold that her doctor told her she might die. Frances responded, "If I am really going, it is too good to be true."

Three years later, she was sick with another cold. After doing all he could, her doctor told her that he wouldn't be seeing her again. "Am I really going this time?" she asked. When the doctor told her that she was, she said, "Beautiful! Too good to be true." A bit later she added: "It's splendid to be so near the gates of heaven."

How does one experience that kind of peace? Frances knew the answer. She firmly believed the words of Isaiah 26:3:

> *You will keep him in perfect peace,*
> *Whose mind is stayed on You,*
> *Because he trusts in You.*

Frances restated that promise in the chorus of her hymn:

> *Stayed upon Jehovah, hearts are fully blest*
> *Finding, as He promised, perfect peace and rest.*

To stay ourselves on the Lord is to rest on Him. It is to lean on Him for support in every situation and circumstance of life.

We should note that the promise in Isaiah 26:3 focuses on the mind. Our minds are to be stayed on God. In other words, our minds are to be supported by His truth. We are to fix and settle our minds on His truth and not allow ourselves to be blown around and carried off by teachings that are opposed to God's truth.

This staying of our minds on God's truth is to be continuous and ongoing. We are to do it on a daily basis. How easy it is for us to wait until a crisis comes up before we stay ourselves on God's truth! Don't wait for a crisis to find peace. Find the peace now, and it will be there for the crisis. And the peace is found by filling our minds with the Word of God.

We often desire certain ends while neglecting the means that lead to those ends. We all desire peace, but do we desire the staying that produces it? If Frances Havergal had a greater supply of peace, it was because she did a better job of staying! If we join with her in her staying, we will be able to join with her in singing:

Like a river glorious is God's perfect peace,
Over all victorious, in its bright increase;
Perfect, yet it floweth fuller every day,
Perfect, yet it groweth deeper all the way.

Stayed upon Jehovah, hearts are fully blest
Finding, as He promised, perfect peace and rest.

Every joy or trial falleth from above,
Traced upon our dial by the Sun of Love;
We may trust Him fully, all for us to do;
They who trust Him wholly find Him wholly true.

Stayed upon Jehovah, hearts are fully blest
Finding, as He promised, perfect peace and rest.

-26-

From God's Word, the Bible...

"Moreover you shall say to them, 'Thus says the LORD:
"Will they fall and not rise? Will one turn away and not return?
Why has this people slidden back,
Jerusalem, in a perpetual backsliding?
They hold fast to deceit, they refuse to return.
I listened and heard, but they do not speak aright.
No man repented of his wickedness, saying, 'What have I done?'
Everyone turned to his own course,
As the horse rushes into the battle.
"Even the stork in the heavens Knows her appointed times;
And the turtledove, the swift, and the swallow
Observe the time of their coming.
But My people do not know the judgment of the LORD."
Jeremiah 8:4-7

The Stork

The white storks fly from South Africa each spring to go to northern Europe. In the fall, they return. More than half a million make this annual journey, soaring as high as 4,000 feet.

One day the prophet Jeremiah was watching the storks. He lived with a broken heart. His people, the citizens of Judah, had turned from the Lord and were living in grievous sin. Jeremiah couldn't take this lightly or casually. Time after time, he pleaded with them to return to the Lord. "Return" is the key word in this prophecy, appearing forty-seven times

As Jeremiah observed the storks flying over his head, he realized that he had been given a sermon. The storks had migrated to other lands, and now they were returning. And here was Jeremiah's sermon: The storks knew enough to return from foreign lands, but the people of Judah didn't know enough to return from sin.

The Bible often uses the animals and birds to drive home spiritual truths. While they are not blessed with the intelligence that we have, they can—and do—serve as our teachers. The truth the stork teaches us is quite clear: We are to return to the Lord when we have strayed from Him. Do we know enough to return to the Lord when we have strayed? Sadly enough, the people of Judah didn't know as much as the stork. If these people had fallen to the ground, they would have had enough sense to get up (v. 4). Now they had fallen spiritually, and they were just lying there, wallowing in the dirt. Jeremiah says they were guilty of "perpetual backsliding."

So we have in Jeremiah's words *a sobering reality*—children of God can indeed stray far from the Lord.

Think about King David of Israel. What a wonderful man! A fearless warrior to fight his people's enemies, an inspired poet to lift their hearts, a visionary leader to plan for their future—that was David. But this was also David—an adulterer, a liar, and a murderer. No, not all the time, but at one time! And that one time was due to him getting far from the Lord.

Think about Simon Peter. One of the original twelve disciples, he walked with the Lord Jesus on a daily basis for more than three years. Oh, the things that Simon Peter saw—the lame made to walk, the deaf made to hear, the blind made to see, three raised from the dead, multitudes fed, storms stilled, demons cast out. We might be inclined to think Simon saw so much that he needed a new set of eyes because one set could only see so much. But it was Simon Peter who denied the Lord Jesus three times on the night before His crucifixion.

We must not think that David and Simon Peter were the only ones who strayed from the Lord. The Bible is dotted with accounts of men and women failing in faith and coming short in obedience.

There is also *a cheering reality* in Jeremiah's words—

children of God can return to the Lord.

There is no sin so great that the Lord can't forgive, and there is no distance so great that it is impossible to return. Jesus made this clear in His parable of the prodigal son (Luke 15:11-24). The young man went very far from home and very deep in sin, but he first came to himself (v. 17) and then he came home to his father (vv. 18-24). Michael Bentley, a Bible commentator, wonderfully observes that God (who is pictured by the father in the parable) never makes returning difficult.

If you are conscious of being away from the Lord and stung by remorse and regret, you may be wondering how it is possible for you to ever return to Him. The prophet Hosea tells you what you must do:

> *Take words with you*
> *And return to the* LORD
> *Say to Him,*
> *"Take away all iniquity;*
> *Receive us graciously …"*
> (Hos. 14:2)

Yes, "take words with you" and come back to the Lord. Tell Him all about your sin and your straying. And rejoice in His forgiveness, which is complete, loving and wholehearted (Hos. 14:4).

-27-

From God's Word, the Bible...

And I said, "This is my anguish;
But I will remember the years of the right hand of the Most High."
I will remember the works of the LORD;
Surely I will remember Your wonders of old.

Psalm 77:10-11

The Language of Yesteryear

How language has changed over the last few decades! Some years ago, someone sent me an email in which he used the computer terms "browsing" and "cookies." Being technologically challenged, I wrote back to say that browsing is something I do in bookstores and cookies are things I eat. I might add that I eat cookies by taking "bites," and there is no letter "y" in bites.

The language of the church has changed over the years as well. I grew up listening to lots of preaching. There was preaching each Sunday morning and evening, preaching in what we called "revival meetings," and preaching in various "youth rallies." It concerns me very much these days that young people in our churches are hearing so little preaching. My estimate is that they are getting about one third of the preaching that I received in my young years.

The preaching I heard in those years used terms that I don't hear much any more. Drawing from such texts as Romans 12:1-2 and 1 John 2:15-17, preachers would often warn us about worldliness, that is, thinking, talking, acting, and dressing like people in modern society—or more simply, the world.

In the small, rural church in which I spent my childhood years, the children would often sing this chorus:

> *Oh, be careful little eyes what you see,*
> *Oh, be careful little eyes what you see;*
> *There's a Father up above,*
> *And He's looking down in love*
> *So, be careful little eyes what you see.*

Subsequent verses dealt with the ears and hearing, the hands and doing, the feet and going, and the mouth and speaking.

A lot of preaching today seems to be directed more toward how we can get along better in the world than it is toward being separate from the world.

The congregation would also sing quite often these lines from Isaac Watts' hymn *Am I a Soldier of the Cross*:

> *Is this vile world a friend to grace,*
> *To help me on to God?*

There was no doubt in Watts' mind about the proper answer:

> *Sure I must fight if I would reign,*
> *Increase my courage, Lord;*
> *I'll bear the toil, endure the pain,*
> *Supported by Thy word.*

That hymn makes me think of another change: We hear little these days about the Christian life as a war and Christians as soldiers. The military metaphor is considered to be politically incorrect and offensive even though the Apostle Paul made much of it (Eph. 6:10-20; 2 Tim. 2:3-3).

We also used to hear a good bit about the danger of backsliding. But the word isn't often spoken in our time.

Backsliding was the term for Christians who were failing to live as they should. Instead of going forward in spiritual things, they were sliding back. Backsliding doesn't mean the Christian ceases to be a Christian. It's possible to fall on the deck of a ship without falling overboard. The backslider is the Christian who has fallen on the deck.

The preachers who used to emphasize the terrible reality of backsliding were faithful to assure us that there is forgiveness and renewal for those who backslide (1 John 1:9).

It was also common years ago to hear pastors and church members speak of various unbelievers as being "under conviction." We understand conviction in the legal realm. It is to be found guilty of breaking the law. It's the same in the spiritual realm. To be "under conviction" means the sinner has become acutely aware that he or she has broken God's law.

Christianity has been reconfigured in our time and presented as a technique for successful living instead of God releasing sinners from the results of their law-breaking through the Lord Jesus Christ. If the law of God is not preached, there will be no conviction of law-breaking, and there will be no fleeing to Christ.

Some might dismiss what I've said as someone merely liking old things, but no teaching is right merely because it's old or because it's new. It is rather a matter of whether it is found in God's Word. Because it is God's Word, it can't change any more than God Himself can change. As we study it, we find that its central theme is the gospel of Christ As the years come and go, that gospel remains the same. It is old, but ever new.

-28-

From God's Word, the Bible...

Alexander the coppersmith did me much harm. May the Lord repay him according to his works. You also must beware of him, for he has greatly resisted our words.

At my first defense no one stood with me, but all forsook me. May it not be charged against them.

But the Lord stood with me and strengthened me, so that the message might be preached fully through me, and that all the Gentiles might hear. Also I was delivered out of the mouth of the lion. And the Lord will deliver me from every evil work and preserve me for His heavenly kingdom.

To Him be glory forever and ever. Amen!

2 Timothy 4:14-18

The Coppersmith and the Lord

On November 5, 2017, a gunman burst into a Baptist church in Sutherland Springs, Texas, and killed twenty-six people, including several children. The two words that went flashing through my mind were "much harm."

Those are the words the Apostle Paul used in connection with Alexander the coppersmith. We know very little about the circumstances to which Paul referred when he wrote: "Alexander the coppersmith did me much harm" (v. 14).

Some commentators think Alexander was instrumental in securing Paul's arrest. Others think he was the leading witness in the prosecution of Paul. Whatever the precise nature of Alexander's role was, it was very damaging for Paul.

If we let Alexander represent harm or evil, we have to say he still lives today.

So where can we find comfort in such a time? The Apostle's words to Timothy enable us to draw four comforting conclusions.

First, *the Lord is not the coppersmith*. In other words, the Lord is not responsible for the evil in this world. Paul says: "Alexander the coppersmith did me much harm." He doesn't say: "The Lord did me much harm." Paul doesn't attribute to the Lord the evil that he had experienced.

Paul doesn't blame the Lord for Alexander's evil because he, Paul, knew that the Lord made everything good. Evil came into this world through Adam and Eve refusing to obey God's commandment, and it has been with us ever since. The true tragedy of human existence is that we decry all the heartaches created by sin while we clutch sin and hold it close to our hearts.

A second comforting conclusion we can glean from Paul's words is cheering indeed—*the coppersmith is not the Lord*. I'm affirming that while evil is alive and well in this world, it will not finally triumph over the Lord.

The coppersmith (evil) could do "much harm" to Paul, but it couldn't keep the Lord from standing with him and strengthening him (v. 17).

Several people have told me over the years that in the harsh difficulties of life, nothing helps them more than remembering that the Lord is with them.

Just how is the Lord with us? He is with us as a sympathizer who understands and cares, as a sustainer who actually gives us strength, grace and wisdom, and as a preserver who keeps our faith from failing.

Third, *the coppersmith also cannot keep the Lord from ultimately delivering His people* (v. 18).

While God allows us to suffer difficulties and trials of various kinds, He will—in His own time and way—bring us through those difficulties. And the greatest deliverance of all is death itself through which the Lord takes us home to heaven where there will be no more pain, sorrow, death or crying.

Fourth, *the coppersmith also cannot keep the Lord from punishing evildoers*. The apostle writes, "May the Lord repay him according to his works" (v. 14). In other words, as one translation puts it, "The Lord will render to him according to his works."

Human justice is imperfect. Much evil goes unpunished in this life. But there is a court of law from which no one will escape. It is God's court. And the justice meted out there will be perfectly fair and right. The only way to be safe on that day is to flee to the Lord Jesus Christ in repentance and faith. On the cross, Jesus took God's just penalty for sin so all who trust Him never have to fear that penalty.

Evil has been with us ever since the beginning of human history, and it will continue to be with us as long as this world lasts. But while evil is ancient, it isn't eternal.

In response to the tragedy in Texas, churches all across the nation started to take security measures. Many are now locking their doors as they worship!

While the evil of this world seems to increase on every hand, believers in Christ look forward to that day when God will put an end to it all and gather His people in heaven. There they will not have to lock the doors as they worship Him because evil itself will have been destroyed, and there they will be free to gaze on Christ in all His glory, free from all fear.

-29-

From God's Word, the Bible...

And He said, "I will certainly return to you according to the time of life, and behold, Sarah your wife shall have a son." (Sarah was listening in the tent door which was behind him.) Now Abraham and Sarah were old, well advanced in age; and Sarah had passed the age of childbearing. Therefore Sarah laughed within herself, saying, "After I have grown old, shall I have pleasure, my lord being old also?"

Now Abraham was one hundred years old when his son Isaac was born to him. And Sarah said, "God has made me laugh, and all who hear will laugh with me."

From Genesis 18:9-15 and Genesis 21:1-7

Laughter, Bad and Good

While these passages are bound together by Sarah's laughter, they are not the same. In the first passage, Sarah's laughter displeased God. In the second, it didn't.

On the first occasion, Sarah laughed with unbelief. The Lord Himself had come to Abraham with wonderful news. Although well advanced in years, he and Sarah would have a son. Listening from inside the tent, Sarah "laughed within herself" (18:12).

She did not believe this promise. It has often been said that if something sounds too good to be true, it probably is. To Sarah this promise was too good to be true.

The Lord didn't share Sarah's amusement. "Why," He asked Abraham, "did Sarah laugh, saying, 'Shall I surely bear a child, since I am old?'" (18:13).

Sarah laughed as if the birth of this son would depend on Abraham and her. The question was not whether the matter was too hard for the two of them. Obviously, it was. The

Lord put the focus where it belonged when He asked: "Is anything too hard for the LORD?" (18:14).

Our faith will always falter if we look to ourselves and our abilities instead of looking to the Lord.

Centuries later, a young Jewish woman was asked to believe something far more difficult than that with which Sarah was presented. Mary was told that she would bear a son who would be conceived without a father. Mary offered a far different response than Sarah. She said to the angel Gabriel: "Behold the maidservant of the Lord! Let it be to me according to your word" (Luke 1:38).

Abraham and Sarah having a son in their old age wasn't the impossible thing. The impossible thing was that God should fail to do what He had promised!

Laughing in response to God's promise, Sarah comes down the corridor of time to warn us about the danger of being unbelieving believers. We also are called to believe things that are hard to believe. God tells us if we want to have forgiveness for our sins and enter into heaven, we must fully rest on His Son dying on a Roman cross! A man dying on a cross! That's the way of salvation? When it seems to be too foolish to believe, we need to recall the words of Paul: "… the foolishness of God is wiser than men, and the weakness of God is stronger than men" (1 Cor. 1:25).

Consider, now, the second episode of Sarah laughing. That which at first seemed impossible to her came gloriously true (21:1-2). When their son was born, Abraham and Sarah gave him the name "Isaac." And what do you suppose the name "Isaac" means? Sarah herself provides the answer: "God has made me laugh, so that all who hear will laugh with me" (21:6).

The name "Isaac" means "laughter." So in the passage we find Sarah laughing again. This time the laughter was okay because it was a different kind. The laughter of unbelief had turned into the laughter of sheer delight over God fulfilling His promise.

This world is one of pain, anguish, heartache, and sorrow. Yes, we laugh in this world, but our laughter is both temporary and tempered. It doesn't go on endlessly, and while it goes on, it is tempered with the burdens and difficulties of life.

All will be different one glorious day. The struggles and sadness of this life will be over. All tears will be wiped away (Rev. 21:4). All skepticism will come to an end.

On that day, God's people will laugh with pure, unadulterated joy. We will laugh with sheer delight that God could love sinners and save them. And we will laugh at ourselves. We will wonder how we could ever have been so foolish as to doubt any of God's promises and how we could ever have been so slow to believe.

The devil tells us now that it's all too good to be true, but it will finally prove to be true because of the powerful, gracious, faithful God that we serve.

-30-

From God's Word, the Bible...

For God so loved the world that He gave His only begotten Son, that whoever believes in Him should not perish but have everlasting life.

Beloved, let us love one another, for love is of God; and everyone who loves is born of God and knows God. He who does not love does not know God, for God is love. In this the love of God was manifested toward us, that God has sent His only begotten Son into the world, that we might live through Him. In this is love, not that we loved God, but that He loved us and sent His Son to be the propitiation for our sins. Beloved, if God so loved us, we also ought to love one another.

John 3:16; 1 John 4:7-11

A Pencil Stub and a Lemon Crate

It was 1917, and young Frederick M. Lehman was working in a citrus packinghouse in Pasadena, California. Financial reversals had brought him to this low point. But Lehman's troubles were not on his mind when he sat on a lemon crate with a pencil stub in his hand. It was something much higher and nobler that occupied his thoughts on this occasion.

That high and noble thing was the love of God. Incredible, isn't it? Here was a young man who was face to face with hardship, but he was thinking about how much God loved him!

So he began to write:

> *The love of God is greater far,*
> *Than tongue or pen can ever tell,*
> *It goes beyond the highest star*
> *And reaches to the lowest hell.*

When the trials of life mount up all around us, we always need to take a good dose of this tonic—the love of God.

But if God loves us, why do we have problems such as financial reversals? The devil always urges us to consult our circumstances to determine whether God loves us. Another hymn-writer, Philip Bliss, urges us to consult the Bible:

> *I am so glad that our Father in heaven*
> *Tells of His love in the book He has giv'n.*
> *Wonderful things in the Bible I see.*
> *This is the dearest that Jesus loves me.*

It's interesting that Bliss wrote this after returning from yet another meeting in which a song had been sung about our love for God. Bliss said, "Let me no more sing about my feeble love for God. Rather let me sing of His great love for me."

Bliss and his wife were killed in an awful train wreck on December 29, 1876. When his trunk arrived home, the words to one of his last hymns were there:

> *I will sing of my Redeemer,*
> *And His wondrous love to me;*
> *On the cruel cross He suffered*
> *From the curse to set me free.*
> *Sing, oh sing, of my Redeemer;*
> *With His blood He purchased me.*
> *On the cross, He sealed my pardon,*
> *Paid the debt and made me free.*

Can we be sure God loves His people? As we read the Bible, we will find it pointing us to Jesus dying on the cross. That Bible and that cross give us the answer most emphatically—Yes! God loves His people. When Satan tells us to look at our difficulties, we must respond by looking in the Bible and looking to the cross.

But back to Frederick on his lemon crate! The first two verses came rather quickly, and then, as is often the case with writing, everything came to a halt. He wanted his song to have three verses, but he couldn't think of another verse. Suddenly, he recalled something from a sermon in which the preacher in soaring oratory had spoken about the love of God. And Frederick had his third verse:

> *Could we with ink the ocean fill*
> *And were the skies of parchment made,*
> *Were every stalk on earth a quill*
> *And every man a scribe by trade.*
> *To write the love of God above*
> *Would drain the ocean dry;*
> *Nor could the scroll contain the whole*
> *Tho' stretched from sky to sky.*

So Lehman didn't just write a third verse; he wrote one of the most wonderful and thrilling of all verses. He essentially says to us: "Do you want to describe God's love? You have before you an impossible task!" Then he adds: "I will give you an ocean full of ink and a sky full of paper. I will make every stalk or reed on earth a writing instrument and every person on earth a writer. So you have your ink, your paper, your writing instruments, and your writers. Now start describing the love of God!"

Then, as it were, Lehman says: "I can tell you before you start where you are going to end. You are going to run out of ink and out of paper before you can complete your task."

Frederick Lehman knew his pencil stub could never convey the greatness of God's love for sinners, but the people of God have been thankful for that stub for many years.

-31-

From God's Word, the Bible...

For I am already being poured out as a drink offering, and the time of my departure is at hand. I have fought the good fight, I have finished the race, I have kept the faith. Finally, there is laid up for me the crown of righteousness, which the Lord, the righteous Judge, will give to me on that Day, and not to me only but also to all who have loved His appearing.

2 Timothy 4:6-8

What a Way to Live! What a Way to Die!

The Apostle Paul knew his time was short when he wrote these words to Timothy. He was in a prison in Rome awaiting the executioner's ax. We might expect him to write morose, sorrowful words. Not Paul! In these verses, he looks in three directions with peace and joy.

First, he looks down at the grave, then back at his life, and forward to eternity. The first look is without fear, the second without regret, and the third without doubt.

Fear, regret, and doubt are cruel tyrants. How much harm and heartache they have caused and continue to cause! To be free from their chains is a marvelous thing indeed. Paul was free. Are we?

He was free from the fear of the grave. There is no trace of terror to be found in the calm words of verse 6. He was ready to die. He refers to it as his "departure." He saw himself pulling up the anchor and setting sail so he could land in another port. What was that other port? Anyone who has passing familiarity with Paul's writings has no difficulty answering. The port in which Paul was going to land was heaven, where he would be with the Lord he loved so very much.

In his letter to the Philippians, Paul spoke of being torn. On one hand, he wanted to continue life in this world so he could continue to preach the gospel. On the other hand, he had an intense desire to "depart and be with Christ." He calls being with Christ "far better" (Phil. 1:23).

How can we face death with Paul's calmness? We must know the Christ that he knew! We must repent of our sins and entrust ourselves completely to the Lord Jesus and what He did for sinners in His life and death.

Paul was also free from regret as he looked back over his life. He saw life as being a fight, a race, and a stewardship, that is, something to be held in trust. More specifically, the stewardship was the Christian faith (Phil. 1:27). Paul was able to say that he had fought the fight, run the race, and kept the stewardship.

Someone might say, "I hope I'm lucky enough to come to the end without any regrets." The way Paul pictures life takes "luck" out of the equation. A fight requires us to discipline ourselves and to put forth effort (2 Tim. 2:4). So does a race (2 Tim. 2:5). And the keeping of a stewardship requires us to discern what is valuable and to protect it with all our might (2 Tim. 1:13). Life to Paul was not a matter of merely existing. It was exerting. The fight was for Christ and against the devil and his forces. The race was for Christ and His cause. The keeping was of Christ and His truth. If we want to die as Paul died, we must live as he lived. We must fight for Christ, run for Christ, and we must serve the truth of Christ.

Finally, *Paul was free from doubt* as he looked ahead (v. 8). Eternity to him was not an uncertain, shadowy thing. Paul knew that he would meet Christ and receive from Him "the crown of righteousness." The Roman government could—and would—pronounce Paul guilty, but the Lord would hand down the verdict "not guilty."

We should note the "will" in Paul's words. "Will" is a word of certainty. It doesn't allow room for doubt. Paul was not merely "crossing his fingers" and hoping for the best.

Paul's certainty regarding eternity was based not on himself and his accomplishments, but rather on the Lord, who is "the righteous Judge." Perhaps someone wonders if the Lord will finally change His mind about letting sinners into heaven, and turn them away. If He were to do so, He would lose more than they would. He has promised that all who repent of their sins and trust in Him and His atoning death on the cross will be forgiven and pardoned. If He were to reverse course at the last minute, He would no longer be righteous. His righteousness ensures that He will keep—and even requires Him to keep—His promises.

So we look at Paul without fear, without regret, without doubt, and we say, "What a way to live! What a way to die!" But if we're wise, we will look even more to the Lord Jesus who made Paul the man he was.

About the Author

Roger Ellsworth is a retired pastor, active in ministry and writing, who lives in Jackson, Tennessee. He and his wife, Sylvia, love the message of the Bible, and they enjoy sharing the wonderful counsel of the Word of God in language that ordinary people can understand and appreciate.

Roger has written numerous books on the Christian faith, and has exercised a preaching ministry for over fifty years. His sermons are available to listen for free on SermonAudio.com.

Coming soon — Book 5: The Day the Milk Spilled

I can't tell you how this saying came about, but I do recall a day when I saw someone crying over spilled milk. The someone wasn't a child. It was my dad. And the milk wasn't the small amount in a glass. It was a lot of milk. For years my parents tried to scratch a living out of a hardscrabble little farm near Mulberry Grove, Illinois. There wasn't much money to be made from farming in those days, at least not from farming on our scale...

Enjoy collecting the My Coffee Cup Meditations Series.

The "Thumbs-Up" Man ISBN 978-0-9988812-5-6
A Dog and A Clock ISBN 978-0-9988812-9-4
When God Blocks Our Path ISBN 978-0-9988812-4-9
Fading Lines, Unfading Hope, ISBN 978-0-9996559-1-7

Enjoy collecting the My Coffee Cup Meditations Series.

The "Thumbs-Up" Man ISBN 978-0-9988812-5-6
A Dog and A Clock ISBN 978-0-9988812-9-4
When God Blocks Our Path ISBN 978-0-9988812-4-9
Fading Lines, Unfading Hope, ISBN 978-0-9996559-1-7

www.mycoffeecupmeditations.com

www.ingramcontent.com/pod-product-compliance
Lightning Source LLC
Chambersburg PA
CBHW070623300426
44113CB00010B/1638